Letters to Kate

sightline books

The Iowa Series in Literary Nonfiction

Patricia Hampl & Carl H. Klaus, series editors

Carl H. Klaus
Letters
to Kate
Life after Life

University of Iowa Press, Iowa City

University of Iowa Press, Iowa City 52242
http://www.uiowa.edu/uiowapress
Copyright © 2006 by Carl H. Klaus
Printed in the United States of America
Design by Richard Hendel

The University of Iowa Press is a member of
Green Press Initiative and is committed to
preserving natural resources.

Printed on acid-free paper

Library of Congress
Cataloging-in-Publication Data
Klaus, Carl H.
    Letters to Kate: life after life / Carl H. Klaus.
        p.   cm.—(Sightline books)
    ISBN 0-87745-971-1 (cloth)
    1. Bereavement.   2. Consolation.   3. Franks,
Kate.   4. Klaus, Carl H.   I. Title.   II. Series.
    BF575.G7K554 2006
    155.9′37′092—dc22   2005051440
    [B]

06   07   08   09   10   C   5   4   3   2   1

That in black ink my love may still shine bright.

—WILLIAM SHAKESPEARE, "Sonnet 65"

Letters to Kate

SATURDAY, NOVEMBER 30

Dear Kate,

This morning — the first time I've been alone all week — I was sitting in your chair in the TV room, thumbing through one of your notepads, and came upon the obituary you'd evidently been drafting for yourself. I remember your saying just a few weeks ago that we had to write our obituaries for the funeral home, but I didn't know you'd been working on one, so I was shocked to find it — as if you had a premonition of things. And surprised to see it was as brief and matter of fact as the one I wrote last Sunday, the day after you died. At least we're still on the same page, though my piece doesn't have the edginess of yours. How could it? Here's a copy of what I wrote, so you can see for yourself:

OBITUARY FOR KATE FRANKS KLAUS

Kate Franks Klaus, 60, of 416 Reno Street, Iowa City, died November 23, 2002, of a stroke at Mercy Hospital.

Kate was born February 26, 1942, in Lisbon, Iowa, to Stuart and Elizabeth Franks. She graduated from Lisbon High School, attended Vassar College, received a B.A. in English from Stanford University, and an M.F.A. in poetry from the University of Iowa Writers' Workshop. Poet, playwright, translator, designer, environmentalist — she co-founded Reno Street Neighborhood Park, as well as Heritage Trees of Iowa City, and the Nancy Seiberling Heritage Grove in Hickory Hill Park. Memorial donations may be made to Heritage Trees of Iowa City, c/o The Civic Center, Iowa City, Iowa. A memorial service will be held in spring at the Nancy Seiberling Heritage Grove.

She is survived by her husband, Carl Klaus, of Iowa City, by her sister Martha Harrington of Largo, Florida, by her brother, John Franks of Denver, Colorado, and by her stepchildren, Amy Klaus Wuellner of Oregon, Wisconsin, Hannah Klaus Hunter of Davis, California, and Marshall Klaus, of Peru, New York.

On another notepad, I found a poem you'd written called "Obit" — one thing leads to another, I guess. But I could hardly believe how bleak it is, even considering your late-night glooms. What made you think that no one would know "just who I was / Just what I did"? Did you imagine yourself living so long as to outlast anyone who might remember you? Or did you really think that no one would care? Whatever the case, I wonder what you'd say about the host of cards and letters I've received — in just a few days, just from people in town. And the comfort food, e-mail, and flowers. Yes, they're consolatory, grieving for my loss. But it's you, Kate, it's you that they're really about — the notes and letters filled with such vivid memories that almost every one of them leaves me in tears. Enough to make up for all my years of tearlessness. Now I know what your mother was going through after your father suddenly died, why she was tearful for so long. Some legacy — your father's stroke to you, your mother's tears to me.

But already I can hear your unmistakable commands: "Enough of the tears. Enough of the mush. Just tell me what happened, and what's been happening since then. And stick to the facts, like the obituary." Easier said than done, Kate. But here it is — just the facts, or nearly so. From start to finish it was less than four hours. You got back from the art fair at one in the afternoon and were dead at twenty to five. So sudden, so swift that it's still impossible to believe. One minute showing me the bowls you'd just bought, your eyes glittering with delight — "Don't you think they'll go perfectly with our dinner plates?" — a few minutes later staring blankly at the oven, a few minutes later staring blankly at me as the milk you were drinking dribbled down the side of your mouth, and a few minutes later, just before the ambulance arrived, tumbling out of your kitchen chair, already paralyzed on one side, else you'd never have fallen like that. Yet still so much in possession of yourself as to worry about our dinner party that evening for Gene, as if your fate were less important than festivities for our weekend guest. How strange, but also how fitting, that your last words to me were about food — "You'll take care of the rice, won't you? And the lamb too?" Our daily sacrament your final concern. Ten minutes later when I arrived at the hospital, you couldn't speak, couldn't move your eyes, and completely lost consciousness when you were having a CT scan. So much for the paramedic's assurance, "Don't worry, all her vital signs are good." Such a massive hemorrhage, "a ten-centimeter bleed, a herniated brainstem," according to the neurologist, that nothing could be done. But just to be sure, I called Amy, given her emergency nursing experience, and she confirmed the doctor's advice — "Don't try to save her, Dad. It's hopeless. Just make sure she gets enough morphine to prevent any pain." So, the last three hours of your life, you lay calmly on your back in an intensive care room, while Gene sat on one side of you and I hovered around the other, sometimes holding your hand, sometimes kissing your forehead, sometimes talking to you, but mostly in such a state of shock (chills coursing down my body nonstop) that I didn't know what to do except not to leave your side, lest you slip away in my absence — as if you weren't already long gone, a million miles away. And when the end did come, I couldn't tell the difference, except that Sarah, the attending nurse, was in tears as she checked your eyes — your beautiful eyes obscured by God knows what fluid — and unhooked the monitor. Your lips still warm when I kissed you goodbye, your body still relaxed when I tried to climb on the gurney. I wanted to hold you, to lie by your side one last time, but it was too narrow for both of us. And the sidebars made me feel like an intruder. So I settled for a clumsy little hug. Such an absurd parting — thirty-seven years together and nothing at the end but a clumsy little hug.

There's more to report, but this is all I can manage right now. I'll try again tomorrow.

SUNDAY, DECEMBER 1

Dear Kate,

Gene left the morning after you died, and ever since I've been thinking how strange that he came to spend that ill-fated weekend with us, after not having seen each other for five years, came because of John's impending death, only to witness yours. When John hired Gene and me as instructors some forty years ago, I never imagined that our lives would intersect in so many ways — on fishing trips, at poker games, professional meetings, and now like this. On the way to the airport, he spoke of being "honored" to be with us when you were dying, whereas I felt blessed by the gift of his calm presence. And dazed by the thought of all he'd been through, given his visit to John and his deathwatch with me. I can hardly imagine what it would have been like without him. At the airport, just before leaving, he gave me a piece of advice I hadn't heard before, but that I've been getting ever since — "Don't make any big decisions about anything for at least a year, not until you're more stable than you are right now."

The way I feel right now, stability is light-years away, especially after last week. An emotional stress test, it began with the sight of your elegant table for the dinner party that never took place, the last work of your hands confronting me and Gene when we got back from the hospital and walked into the dining room — the green silk runner down the length of the table, the green glass centerpiece with the chrysanthemums still as fresh as when you arranged them, the green straw placemats, the green napkins atop the brown pottery plates, the wood-handled cutlery, the amber wine glasses, the amber water glasses. I remember you putting it together that morning, still in your nightgown, swanning around the dining room before you went to the fair — remember you showing me the moss green mums and telling me, with a twinkle in your eye, "They're called Kermits." But the shock of your death was so huge, obliterating, that I completely forgot the dinner party, the table, and everything else until Gene and I walked into the house that afternoon. Such a dazzling emblem of your impeccable eye, I was momentarily transfixed by it, then overcome with remorse for having taken such things for granted. Then and there, I vowed to leave the table untouched as long as possible, to keep the flowers alive as long as possible, to celebrate Thanksgiving — some thanksgiving! — on a table set by you. And that's what happened five days later, with a guest list of your dreams. Not only Marybeth, Ken, and Elizabeth, in keeping with our neighborly rotation, but also Amy, Hannah, Marshall, and Martha — the first time that my children and your sister were all here together in at least ten years. The only one missing was you. But you were there — and not just in the setting and your classic menu, nor just in the simple toast "To Kate." You were there in the "Thanksgiving Prayer" that I found among your papers on the kitchen counter.

Lord, we thank you for the harvest
Spread before us,
And the company of loved ones
All around us.

Such a haunting little grace that I barely got through it. But then again, everything the past week has been so haunting that I barely got through it. Like going to the funeral home last Sunday, almost a year to the day after you dragged me there to make arrangements for ourselves. "We've got to do this," you said, "so it's all taken care of when the time comes, and no one has to worry about what to do or what we want." Too bad you didn't tell them how to do your hair — not to rinse out the gray, not to comb out the bangs. But the strange-looking hairdo was nothing compared to the feel of your body under the lovely antique quilt — so stiff and cold when I bent over to hug you that the chills swept over me again, and words came rushing out of my mouth as if some other voice had commandeered my own. "That's not her, that's not her," I screamed, running out of the room. And Carolyn, the funeral attendant, answered me calmly, frankly — "No, it's not her, it's not her at all. That's just her body. She's gone." A truth that suddenly hit me so hard, I burst into tears for the first time since you died, the dam broken at last that had me wondering until then whether I was so numb, so stunned, I'd never shed a single tear.

I've heard about people being in shock or suffering from post-traumatic stress, but I never imagined it could be so weird. Like the sirens ringing in my ears, the chills sweeping down my body again and again the first night in bed without you. And the night after that and the night after that, until Amy gave me a sedative that smoothed out the nights a bit but certainly not the days. Now, in fact, I suddenly find myself breaking down almost any time or place — in the supermarket aisle with Marshall the day before Thanksgiving, in the garden yesterday afternoon pulling the last of our fall radishes, in the kitchen this evening, looking out at the candles that someone's evidently been lighting in memory of you at the neighborhood park, at the end of the new Harry Potter movie when the young heroine, seemingly dead, suddenly came to life again. A fantasy too close to home.

Were it not for our friends and neighbors, I might have been in tears all week, but their visits and gifts made me feel as if I should put up a staunch front, as you would have done, as your mother did after your father's sudden death. What else to do, then, but tell them the story of that fateful afternoon, the story they evidently craved to know, as if knowing what happened could make sense of your shocking death. I told it so many times that my tale hardened into a set piece — "It all began just a few minutes after she got home from the art fair . . ." How quickly a formula takes hold — life and death alike embalmed in language. And when I wasn't telling the story, I was showing photographs of you that I propped up around the living room. The big black-and-whites that Rowley took in my bachelor apartment when we were still in our salad days and he needed to do a series of portraits for his photography class. You sitting at the ice cream table in your wide-brimmed hat, holding a large umbrella over your head, your fingers elegantly clutching the handle. You sitting at the table, your eyes cast downward, your hand on its marble surface, your shoulder-length hair covering half your face. What a bizarre yoking — the afternoon of your death and an afternoon thirty-seven years ago when you came to my apartment and modeled for Rowley's art shots. But then again, compared to your death, nothing seems bizarre. Not even these letters.

MONDAY, DECEMBER 2

Dear Kate,

Your clothes were also part of the story last week, but I didn't say anything yesterday, for I couldn't say it all in just a few words. So here's a rundown of what happened. A few days after you died, I looked in your closet and was swept away by the sight of all your things, suddenly beside the point without you to fill them. Such an absurd spectacle, I asked Amy, Hannah, and Martha to take what they wanted and box up the rest for the Goodwill Store and Salvation Army. How strange it felt to make that request, for I always assumed you'd be dealing with my personal effects. And why not? You're ten years younger than me, so you should have outlived me by at least ten years. And grieved for me, rather than I for you. And wept over my clothes, as I have wept over yours. Such a mess of self-indulgent feelings that I could see myself turning into a wet dishrag, or a closet fetishist, if I didn't get rid of your stuff. And who better to do the sorting than my daughters and your sister. Besides, I thought you'd want me to "spread things around," the way you always did when you went through your clothes each year. But I couldn't bring myself to part with everything just like that. Especially not your handmade outfits — so elegantly designed and tailored that I plan to keep them awhile in the oak wardrobe, before giving them to the Women's Archives. Do you see how torn I was — how torn I am! — about letting go of things? Even your extravagant shoe collection — now all gone except for a pair of black clogs mistakenly left behind — even your shoes, or the mere thought of them, fill me with longing. I wish they were still here, rivaling Imelda's. So perhaps you can see how hard it was just to stick my head in our bedroom when they were going through your drawers and closet. A four-day ordeal that ended with everything empty, except for the inside of the closet door, where your lavender housejacket was hanging. When I mentioned it to Hannah, she said, "We thought you should keep it, Dad," and I understood why the next morning when I got up and it took me by surprise and I hugged it like a rag doll. Now I expect to keep it there as long as I live, and not as a fetish, but as a reminder of what you looked like when you came downstairs for your morning orange juice and coffee. "Complacencies of the peignoir." I've also kept your silk scarves, so friends and neighbors can choose something special for themselves. Your wide-brimmed hats are still atop the pie safe, your Ben Franklins still by the bedside, and all your summer things still in the steamer trunk where you put them just a few weeks ago, ready for our trip to Hawaii.

Everything's where it should be except for Jag, who limped downstairs this morning after a week of hiding out in the attic and the backyard, grieving I'm sure for you. I thought at first that his limp might be another sign of grief until I noticed a bruise over his eye, took him into the vet's, and discovered that he was evidently hit by a car. Grieving indeed! Bill says he'll be fine after several days at the clinic, but it looks like he nearly spent all of his nine lives at once. With Jag out of the house, I thought it would be a good time to bring Puck back home again. He's been at the vet's ever since we took him in the day before you died — so many people coming in and out of the house last week he'd have been even more hyper than usual. But today he's been very calm, especially after I took him for a long walk in the cemetery. I wonder if he knows that you're missing. How could he not, having spent so many nights in your lap?

TUESDAY, DECEMBER 3

Dear Kate,

Early this morning I saw you again — in a dream. Better a dream than nothing. It began with someone dropping me off in front of the house. A light was on in the kitchen but otherwise the place was completely dark, and the same outside, except for a snow flurry, the flakes blowing and swirling like they are right now. I trudged up the driveway, my feet crunching against the gravel, the wind so hard it slowed me down until I turned the corner of the house, walked up to the back porch, looked in the window of the back door, and there you were, right behind the window, waving an arm above your head, a big smile, an impish smile on your face, your lips moving as if to say, "Surprise, Surprise! I'm here, I'm here!" But no sooner did I see you than I awoke, heart beating, chills sweeping down my body, and a sirenlike noise ringing in my ears, the same noise I heard the first few nights after you died.

When Trudy called from New Jersey this evening, I told her about my dream, and she was elated — "How lucky you are, how lucky to see her so soon!" Such a dear friend that she's worrying about me even though she's in a vigil for her mother, stricken a few days ago by a heart attack. So I didn't tell her how I went back to sleep, hoping to see you again, and got nothing but another sudden awakening, with all the traumatic sensations. I'm beginning to feel like Pavlov's dog.

I did see you again — and feel you again — late this afternoon when Carolyn delivered your ashes. I couldn't just take the box and send her away, so I invited her in for a glass of cider, and then showed her some pictures of you that I've pulled out over the last several days — in the kitchen, in your perennial bed, in the backyard with Martha, on the Kalalau Trail in Hawaii, on the Yangtze River with me. I wanted her to see what you really looked like — in life rather than death — then showed her how you had restored the downstairs, stripped all the woodwork, decorated the rooms, designed the gazebo, landscaped the backyard, and so on. I wanted her to see you in all your guises before it came time for her to open the box. By then it was five thirty, nearly dinnertime, and there was no putting it off any longer, so I got your grandmother's black flower vase from the corner of the living room, brought it out to the kitchen counter, removed the dried statice from your perennial bed that you put in the vase several weeks ago, and suggested that we put your ashes in there, topped by the statice. It seemed like exactly the sort of place you'd like, until I scatter them on your perennial bed this spring.

The minute I set the vase on the counter, she opened the box, pulled out a clear plastic bag containing the ashes, and I suddenly felt an intense shudder ripple down my entire body. And then a great heaving and sobbing overtook me as I began to feel the bag and fondle it, telling her again and again how final and definitive it was. "Yes," she said, "she's gone, but she's still all around you in all she's done to make this such a beautiful place, and she's still in your thoughts, and always will be." Sweet and well-meaning words, and for the most part true, but words I've heard so many times the past several days that I've begun to feel like a connoisseur of griefspeak. Just then, I couldn't resist putting my hands in the bag, feeling your ashes, sifting them through my fingers, and I was surprised by the silkiness. Oh yes, there were little bits and pieces that hadn't been completely reduced to ash, but most of your remains were — and are — so fine, so silky, so powdery they left a pale gray film on my hands.

WEDNESDAY, DECEMBER 4

Dear Kate,

I was doing the bills this morning, when I came on a couple of checks payable to you, and didn't know what to do. So I called Dan and after the usual condolences — always the usual condolences — he switched into his lawyerly mode and said I could deposit the checks but should keep a record for future reference. He also assured me that our joint ownership of the house means that your half of it automatically passes to me. But when I told him about the investments for your nieces and nephews, he said we'll probably have to probate your estate and told me that he needed to see your will. "You've got it," I said. "No," he said, "I only have a copy — I need to see the original, and you've got it." Original? Photocopy? I couldn't help wondering what difference it makes. I also wondered where the original might be, for I assumed it was on file with Dan, and when I looked in your desk, the only thing there was a photocopy. Then I called Sue at the bank, and asked if I could make the change in your investments that you and I discussed a few weeks ago. So, as your trusty trust officer, she also wants to see the will, to make sure I'm the executor, in which case the bank will make the changes that I recommend. Will, will, will — I'm beginning to feel the force of your will as never before, and the will of the legal establishment too. I mean, what's the point of making photocopies if the original is the only will that matters? And what if I can't find the original? What then? Is your will in a state of indefinite suspension? A legal limbo without recourse? Or does the legal establishment have a legal escape mechanism for this as for all contingencies? Stay tuned for further developments.

THURSDAY, DECEMBER 5
Dear Kate,

Every day this week, I'm having lunch or dinner with one of our friends — so many invitations that I feel like a social butterfly. But the flurry of invitations will probably dry up so quickly that I'll wish I hadn't been worrying about it. Still, I can't help feeling there's something wrong with my going out like this so soon after your death, especially when I think of your mother's lonely vigil in the wake of your father's death. Maybe it's also my childhood memory of how we all wore black armbands for several months after my uncle Manny died, but something deep within makes me feel as if I'm breaking a taboo. Yet it's hard to say no, and not just because I don't want to turn away our friends, but also because I don't want to spend my days and nights alone without any kind of companionship. You'd know exactly what to do in this situation, and you'd do it without all this fretting. Isn't it ridiculous — I'm seventy years old and don't know how to behave without you.

Speaking of etiquette, now that I've become a student of grieftalk, I can tell you that "How're ya doin'?" (with an earnest look to match) is usually the first thing people ask when they see me. And why not? It's a natural question. But I've answered it so often that I now find

myself automatically reverting to a canned response — "Well, sometimes I can keep myself distracted enough with this and that (household chores, the monthly bills, e-mail, TV) that I don't think about it,
but sometimes, and there's no predicting when, the full horror of it,
the magnitude of it all, descends upon me, and then the tears come
welling up, and then . . ." And then they often reply with a now familiar response. "Of course, of course, and crying is an important part of
grieving, of working your way through this terrible loss." And when I
tell them about writing you these letters, a strange look often flits
across their face, and they tell me it's a good thing to be doing, "a good
way of keeping in touch." Or words to that effect. Sometime, perhaps,
I'll get up the nerve to tell them about writing without any hope of
response.

FRIDAY, DECEMBER 6

Dear Kate,

At the bank this morning, Sue looked at a photocopy of your
will, saw that it named me beneficiary and executor, and agreed to my
choosing your investments. That done, I authorized her to sell your
current holdings and replace them with one of the real-estate investment trusts that I told you about a few weeks ago — a stock that stands
a good chance of doubling over the next several years, so each of your
nieces and nephews will get the twenty thousand that you hoped to
give them. Such a good start to the day that I should have known it was
a false lead. The bad news came just a few minutes later, when I went
through everything in the safe deposit box and couldn't find the original of your will, which makes me wonder what Dan will do when I see
him next Tuesday.

And it wasn't any better when I checked the answering machine and
heard a cheery little message from Holly — "Just calling to say hi and
hope you're doing well. I'm standing here looking out over Lake
Michigan. Lain and I are heading back to Iowa City this afternoon
and look forward to seeing you soon." Such an attentive friend — she
never misses a chance to buck me up, even when she's out of town.
But I wonder if she realized that you and I were scheduled to be in Chicago this next weekend, and we too were supposed to be looking out

over the lake — from the Navy Pier and the Chicago Shakespeare Theater. The minute I heard her message I thought of your now prescient
refrain: "Don't you realize how little time we have?"

I thought of that refrain again at Carol's this evening, given how
little time she and Pierre had together. Though our offices were side by
side all these years, I never realized until now how painful it must have
been for her when he died just as suddenly as you, and she was left with
three young children to raise and classes to teach as well. Compared to
her, I considered myself fortunate to be free of such burdens, until she
told me they were a blessing. Which made me think that perhaps I
need something to do beside writing these letters, something pur-
poseful to keep me busy and keep my mind off things. But then again,
I don't want to lose touch, as I have the last few days, unable to con-
jure you up, hear your voice, smell your skin, feel you next to me.
Which moved Carol to tell me that she "didn't change the sheets for
several weeks after Pierre died, so I could still smell him beside me."
Too bad that Martha changed the sheets on our bed the day after she
arrived — too bad your sister is a housecleaning freak. I told that to
Carol, and we had a good laugh over the sheets and the escapades of
colleagues in the backward abysm of time when we were all so young
it seemed as if we would live forever. Which made me think of your refrain again. And again.

SATURDAY, DECEMBER 7
Dear Kate,

This morning I made a return visit to the hospital with gifts for
Sarah, who took such good care of you at the end. I gave her one of
your sweaters and a matching necklace, also copies of my gardening
memoirs, so she can read about you, and a thank-you note on one of
your daffodil cards. Getting my gifts together on this sunny morning,
I felt so good about myself — 'tis better to give than to receive — that
I never imagined what it might be like to go back there again until I entered the intensive care unit, saw the room where you died, and suddenly was overwhelmed with the memory of it all. Sarah was sitting behind a long desk, chatting with colleagues, and didn't recognize me at
first. Then, "Oh, I remember you," her face turning slightly red, her
eyes a bit watery, as she asked me the now familiar question, "How are

you doing?" I don't remember what I told her, but I do remember her saying again and again, "Oh, that's so sweet of you," as I gave her the sweater and necklace, and "I'm a gardener too," as I gave her the books, and "Oh, these are wonderful," as I showed her some pictures of you so she could see what you looked like in life rather than death. By then we were both on the verge of tears, and I didn't know what to say — what can one ever say? — so I took my leave with a quick thank-you and headed off to Bunny's pottery sale. Going there without you was another heavy trip, but Amy and Hannah asked for bowls, platters, or other serving pieces for Christmas, and it's so rare that my daughters ever ask for anything that I could hardly refuse. So out to his place I went, the roll and sweep of the winter farmland bright beige in the sun, exactly the way you always like it this time of year. Beautifully, achingly sere. And it wasn't any better when I came upon the creekside spot where we used to take the groundhogs and possums in the Havahart trap. But I did find a good bowl and matching ladle for Amy, and Bunny didn't ask how I'm doing, so that was a plus of sorts. Too bad I didn't take my leave as quickly as with Sarah. For when I asked what he was up to, Bunny told me at length about a recent trip to China — he's studying ancient pottery kilns — and that, of course, brought back memories of our Yangtze River cruise a few years ago. Maybe I shouldn't ask people about their doings, just as I hope they'll not inquire about mine, for their answers so often connect with something in our lives that every conversation is like a time bomb, wired to explode in my face.

SUNDAY, DECEMBER 8

Dear Kate,

A cat was flaked out on the porch last night when I got home from taking Puck for his bedtime walk. I knew it wasn't Jag, because he was inside recuperating from his stay at the vet's. But it sure looked like him, especially the hump of gray fur. It was a dark night, and the porch was unlit, so I couldn't identify the critter, until I bent down to stroke its body, saw a long furless tail, and suddenly realized that the cat was, in fact, a possum. A possum that had evidently been dining on a bag of dried bread cubes that I stored outside last week to cut down on the overflow of food from Thanksgiving. When I saw the bag next to the possum, I also realized what had happened to the other bread cubes that disappeared two days ago. But my pleasure at connecting the dots was nothing compared to my distress about what to do with the possum, its body limp, its jaw dangling open, saliva oozing from its mouth — evidently dead from having eaten something poisonous. I didn't want to touch it again, but I definitely wanted to get it off the porch. So I pulled out the push broom from behind the settle and swept the possum down the stone steps, across several feet of the terrace, until it was well under the yew bush and beyond the reach of Puck's leash. I planned to crate it up and dispose of it this morning. But this morning, believe it or not, the beast was gone. Completely gone. Talk about playing possum! That was better even than the one that played dead a few years ago when I was taking it out to the countryside.

Sometimes when I wake up in the morning, my head still foggy with sleep, I imagine that you've been playing possum, and when I open my eyes I'll find you curled up on your side of the bed, just where you should be.

MONDAY, DECEMBER 9
Dear Kate,

Today was a day of firsts — the first since you died that I spent entirely at home, the first that I had all three meals alone at home, and the first of my new regimen, which I established the minute I got out of bed. The regimen, as you'll see, is nothing special, just a way of getting myself back on schedule. Though I haven't said anything about it in these letters, the embarrassing truth is that I've been staying in bed later and later every morning, sometimes not getting shaved, dressed, and ready for the day until it's almost time for lunch. The sure sign of a fellow in retreat, adrift in the backwaters of his grief. A far cry from my rise and shine in days of yore. And my mealtimes have been just as bad, noshing out of the icebox, rather than sitting down to a carefully prepared dinner as we did all our lives together. Breaking bread alone is a real drag, as you know from the times when I was consulting. And now I've been getting a taste of what you went through, dining with only the animals for company, Puck by the kitchen table waiting for handouts, Jag on the sidelines waiting for Puck to be gone. The only difference, of course, is that you knew I'd return. Bereft of such knowledge, I've had no choice but to decree a new regimen for myself, as follows: (1) get up in time to put Jag and Puck out for their morning constitutionals no later than seven; (2) linger in bed, reading and musing, no later than eight; (3) shower, shave, and be ready for breakfast each morning no later than nine; (4) make the bed each morning before coming down for breakfast; (5) prepare all meals as carefully as if Kate were still alive; (6) choose a good book or magazine for companionship while dining. Isn't it pathetic that I have to put these things in writing to be sure of keeping myself in line? On the other hand, lest you think I've reformed, the sheets haven't been changed and the wash hasn't been done since Martha was here. "Growing up," as you used to say (or sing) in that plaintive tune of yours, "is so hard to do." Even so, the rewards of Boy Scout orderliness, not to mention the keen sensations of self-righteousness, are enough to make a believer of me — at least for the time being.

TUESDAY, DECEMBER 10

Dear Kate,

I dreamt of you again last night. This time, we were visiting someone here in town, and you were a special guest, invited to talk about the Heritage Trees project. I was standing at one end of a large living room, chatting with a few people. You were at the other end of the room, a faint smile on your face, seemingly about to offer a few remarks, when suddenly you disappeared — poof! — just like that. A blank space where you'd previously been standing. I waited and waited for you to reappear, wondering what had become of you, where you had gone, and then awoke, with the realization that I was waiting in vain. And my distress was at the flood. But now looking back, I wonder how I could be taken in by so obvious a dream, especially given its transparent similarity to my back-porch dream of last week. Here one moment, gone the next. Then again, I'm fascinated and appalled by how cunningly my dreams have simplified and whitewashed your demise, especially when I remember that awful moment when I walked over to where you were standing by the wall oven, tapped you on the shoulder, and you turned around, looked at me with the most tender look in your eyes that I'd ever seen, which suddenly gave way to the most pained look in your eyes that I'd ever seen, which suddenly gave way to the most distant look in your eyes that I'd ever seen, and said plaintively, "Will you please tell me something funny?" A voice coming from somewhere else, so completely unlike your own, that it sounded as if you'd suddenly been possessed by an alien being. In retrospect, I've come to think that your swift transformations just then must have been occasioned by the terrible inner workings of the hemorrhage. And the blank, unfocused look in your eyes, a sure sign that you were going blind. How terrified and alone you must have been, for though I was there to hold you and call 911, we were miles apart, and the distance widening with every second. I couldn't even think of anything funny to tell you I was so distraught at the sight of what you were going through. As if something dark, unspeakably dark and mysterious, had taken hold of you, as indeed it had. "O dark, dark, dark, amid the blaze of noon. Irrecoverably dark!"

WEDNESDAY, DECEMBER 11

Dear Kate,

So many cards and letters the past two weeks that they fill the huge bowl we bought from Bunny a few years ago. My cup runneth over. I'm alone and not alone, and the confusion is sometimes dizzying. The letters that came this afternoon were vividly detailed, so rich with memories and intense feeling that they make me wonder once again how you could possibly have thought that no one cared. They also make me wonder whether I can bring myself to answer them all. And worse still, they make me wonder why I haven't been more consoling when others have died. When Trudy called this afternoon — her mother's still hanging on — she told me about the cards and letters that came in the wake of her father's death, how "incredibly comforting" they were. "Like a blessing," she said. And I understood what she meant, though I also had to admit that until now I would never have believed they could make such a profound difference. How strange that I, a so-called writer and sometime writing teacher, would be so late in realizing that when everything else is gone, words and memories matter more than ever before. Why else am I writing you these letters?

THURSDAY, DECEMBER 12

Dear Kate,

At Dan's office this morning, everything worked out much better than I expected. He won't have to probate your will, given the bank's willingness to turn over your investments to me. And, despite his disclaimers of last week, he did find the original of your will in his files, exactly where I thought it was. So, after all, I'm not losing my mind or any of our important documents. But I did lose control of myself right in the middle of a breezy conversation at the end of our business, when I suddenly realized, and blurted out, that I now have more money than ever before — all the money you'd have needed to outlive me for twenty or thirty years — and nothing I care to spend it on, nothing. I'd sooner be bankrupt, I told him, if it would bring you back to life. And then the tears came welling up, while Dan stood there at a loss for words except to say, "Of course, of course." Of course. Such an embarrassing outburst that I apologized and ducked out of his office, wondering how often he has to deal with teary widowers, wondering also how long I'm going to be one. I thought about that this afternoon, when the mail brought a letter from the hospital, inviting me to take part in an eight-session therapy project for people in grief. But I couldn't imagine myself doing group therapy anymore than you ever could when you were recovering from cancer. And certainly not in so brief a span as eight sessions. On the other hand, it's clear that I need something to get myself under control, as I discovered when I picked up the Jeep this afternoon, and it felt so good that I couldn't wait to get home so you could try it yourself. The thought of which undid me until I noticed the gas gauge on empty — unfilled since you topped off the tank the morning before you died.

When Holly called this afternoon, she told me that I seem to be putting so good a face on things that she and others are worried I might be deluded into thinking I can get over this quickly and easily. So I told her about today and that set her mind at ease. How strange, that I have to assure people I'm grieving enough. As in, Don't worry, world, I'm going crazy, it's just that I keep it to myself — I'm a Gemini. Like at David's this evening, I brought a bowl of saffroned rice and amused him with the tale of how I made it for our first date and you loved me forever after. Too bad Rebecca was off doing ministerial duties, so she didn't hear the story of my miraculous rice. But David distracted me with news from the nonfiction program, which he's now directing. Such a loyal colleague and friend that I did my best to be of good cheer. I'm a Gemini.

FRIDAY, DECEMBER 13

Dear Kate,

Remember how I often wished for dreams like yours? Vivid, action-packed, in Technicolor? Now, at last, it's beginning to look like I've inherited yours, thanks to my yearning or mourning or letter writing (or all of the above). How else to account for the fact that I dreamed of you again last night — in other words, three times now since you died, whereas I can't recall myself ever having dreamt of you when you were alive. Can't even recall having dreamt (or remembered my dreams) more than a few times a year. So it seems as if you've taken up residence in the flickering, fleeting realm of my nighttime visions. A life after death in dreamland. Last night's dream went on for so long — or so it seemed — and was so convincing that I took it for granted you were still here, and only realized the delusion when I woke up and saw you weren't beside me in bed. But the dream was momentarily so intriguing that I lay there, puzzling over its significance.

Do you remember how we were always misplacing things the past few years — me my car keys, you your glasses? Well, this time in my dream it was the checkbook, and no matter where I looked — upstairs, downstairs, inside, and out, in your purse, on the counter, in my pocket, in my jacket, in the Jeep — I couldn't find it, couldn't find it anywhere, and neither could you. An anxiety dream, par excellence. But this time you didn't chide me or tell me to get my head in the game. You just looked at me very calmly and assured me very sweetly that it would eventually turn up. "Not to worry," you said, and only now in the process of writing about it do I realize what occasioned the dream. Namely, my inability to find the checkbook in the days shortly after you died, though I looked in all the likely places. But a few days later, when I realized that it might be in the clothes you were wearing the day you died, I looked into the bag of your things that I brought home from the hospital and found it, just as you assured me in the dream. In other words, the dream was a virtual replay of a lost-and-found episode that took place during the week after you died, an episode I'd completely forgotten in the crush of experience since then, but that now seems like an emblematic form of guidance, thanks to your comforting advice. With dreams like that, I could easily become an addict.

SATURDAY, DECEMBER 14

Dear Kate,

Saturday, once my favorite, now the day from hell, and it ran so true to form that I might send a copy of this report to Holly, so she can tell the world I'm grieving aplenty. Probably the result of Christmas shopping without you. No wonder I feel like Scrooge before his conversion. And evidently look like him too, judging from the remark of a salesclerk, who said she'd gift-wrap my packages, "but only if you can replace that scowl with a smile." And it wasn't just the shopping. It was lunch downtown without you and the spectacle of a young couple at a table in front of me. She in blue jeans, leather boots, and crisply ironed shirtwaist, two or three buttons discreetly opened to show her chest but not her bra or her breasts, just the way you did in your salad days — also hazel eyes like yours, skin almost as pale as yours, and sleek as you back then. She didn't really look like you, but in all too many ways she reminded me of you when we first met. And her companion, a handsome mestizo, didn't look at all like me, but reminded me of myself back then. Looking intently at each other, talking across their sandwiches, making plans, it seemed, if only for the day. Though I wish them well, I wish I had never seen them, especially when I was dining alone trying to enjoy my split pea soup and spinach salad. No more dining out alone. Also no more sorting through pictures of you, as I discovered late this afternoon, especially when listening to romantic piano concertos. But then again, I broke down on my way out of Fin and Feather, and when I misplaced my gloves in Dillard's, and when I discovered the burners still on an hour after I cooked dinner. All of which makes me think that Trudy must have been right when she told me there's no predicting a run of breakdowns, that when they come, they come, especially when you're in an emotionally vulnerable place, as I seem to be right now. If this is what Christmas has in store, I wonder what's coming for New Year's.

SUNDAY, DECEMBER 15

Dear Kate,

Just back from my afternoon walk with Puck, the cemetery route as usual, and I couldn't help thinking how much it's changed in the past few weeks — the terrain I've been blithely trespassing all these years, as if it were a scenic extension of our backyard, now suddenly more fraught with significance than ever before. Death, it seems, has a way of putting everything in perspective.

And not just a cemetery. This afternoon in the cemetery, for example, I suddenly remembered how grief-stricken I felt some forty years ago, when I was newly divorced from Meredith. A death of sorts, or so it seemed, especially after eleven years of marriage and three children. What else could I think, reduced to living alone in a little apartment, with an income so small that I could hardly imagine myself residing someday in a big, old home on a spacious lot, blessed with the beauty of your perennial borders and the bounty of my vegetable beds. Beyond the wildest dreams of my orphaned childhood, but now so barren without you, that my desolate situation back then seems palmy by comparison, especially since you were in the future rather than the past. Oh, how I moped back then, endlessly listening to André Previn's poignant arrangements of Jerome Kern, when I should have been upbeat with Gershwin, celebrating an abundant lifetime to come. A life after death that anyone might prize, except for this turn of events. So now I wonder what the future might hold, other than looking back.

MONDAY, DECEMBER 16

Dear Kate,

I took the Jeep in first thing this morning and had all four tires replaced — you were right about their treads wearing down. So I'm "ready to hit the road," as the service manager told me on my way out. The only problem is there's no place I care to go without you behind the wheel. But people continue to ask me, "Are you going somewhere for the holidays?" Or, "Are you planning to leave town for awhile?" As if travel could take me someplace where the memory of you, the thought of you, might not exist. An island paradise called Amnesia, a place completely free of grief. Wouldn't it be nice to go there? Then I wouldn't remember that we were supposed to be coming home today from Chicago, and I wouldn't recall our train ride two years ago, when your ankle was in a cast and we ate in the dining car, reveling in a winter snowstorm. And I wouldn't remember how you always spent these mid-December days at the dining room table, surrounded by tubes of wrapping paper, spools of ribbon, sheets of labels, rolls of bubble wrap, and garbage bags full of plastic peanuts — Santina's workshop — boxing up presents in time for everyone in California, Colorado, Florida, Hawaii, New Jersey, New York, North Carolina, Wisconsin, and God knows where else. But in truth, I could hardly forget your Christmas doings, trapped as I was in your workshop the past two days, trying to do things up as amply and artfully as you, complete with a jar of your June jam in every box. Talk about tears, I felt like a sentimental hero in a Dickensian tale for contemporary readers. And it wasn't any better when I went to the back hallway to look for some Scotch tape and stumbled on your favorite sunhat, the one you'd been looking for last winter when we went to Hawaii, the one that sits atop your head in all the garden and vacation shots of the past twenty-five years. Now I now why people talk about the holidays being a difficult time for people in grief. But the worst of it today was when I returned a call from Trudy, whose mother is now unconscious, on the verge of death, but yesterday was evidently alert enough not only to say her goodbyes but also to thank everyone for taking good care of her. A wonderful story in its way, except that it made me think of how we didn't have a chance to say goodbye.

TUESDAY, DECEMBER 17
Dear Kate,

Today, for the first time in three weeks, the mail didn't bring any cards or letters — not surprising, given the hundreds of people who've already written or sent memorial contributions to the civic center. A welcome break from the daily run of condolences, sometimes so many each day that I can hardly bear to read them all. It's a strange thing how such well-meant expressions of sympathy can become the source of unintended pain, keeping one's grief as green as a rainforest. Just a week or so ago, I remember their being such a comfort that I read some to Trudy over the phone, but now even a tin of Christmas cookies is bittersweet, reminding me of the stars and moons and trees you made with your old-fashioned cookie cutters, and how we iced them in bright colors and delivered them to friends and neighbors.

Sometimes I think of you so much that I completely lose track of things. Like this morning, I wrote a Christmas card to Trudy, to accompany the Native American brooch you bought in Vancouver — I think it'll give her a boost, especially given her love of silver jewelry. But I misplaced our address book, though I had it right beside me when I was writing the letter. Up and down the stairs I went, at least four times, each time checking all the obvious spots on each floor, on the verge of tears and screaming, until I accidentally discovered it lying open on the attic desk, where I put it when I was looking for something else. "Slow down, slow down," said I to myself. "Remember what Kate said about keeping your head in the game." And with that in mind, I headed off to lunch with Sue, only to discover that I forgot to bring her the bank forms. I wonder if grief counselors have a term for this — displacement? dislocation? distraction? Whatever the word, it probably begins with "dis," as in "to undo."

This evening, I came upon your coats still hanging in the downstairs closet. The brown salt-and-pepper tweed that took me back to the fall when we first met, and you were wearing one just like it. And the dark blue dress coat that made you look like the classiest thing in Iowa City. What a joy it was to hug you in those coats, to feel you within them, like a sleek creature inside its fur.

WEDNESDAY, DECEMBER 18

Dear Kate,

Ever since you died, I've been getting more and more uneasy about the things of yours that have come into my hands. Please notice that I've deliberately avoided the word "possession," for though I've inherited all your stuff — clothes, jewelry, paintings, quilts, stocks, books, bookcases, and so on — I don't feel as if they're mine, don't feel anything like ownership. How could I possibly own things so distinctively yours, like your shell collection, things you acquired over a lifetime of being who you are. Worse still, how can I lay claim to stuff you inherited from your parents and grandparents. I felt that quite keenly this afternoon when I went to the corner cupboard to get a wine glass for dinner, and there on the top shelf right above our clear glass goblets were the amber goblets, cups, fruit cups, saucers, and dessert plates from your grandmother Orlie — she of the Victorian migraines and morals, whose fabled world of white gloves and drawn curtains was so distant from mine it seems outlandish that her goblets should be cohabiting with mine. And I'm sure she would feel the same way, thank you. But it's not just a matter of profound cultural and personal difference that makes me uneasy. No, there's also something deeply existential that's at stake. And the only way I can suggest the problem is to say that I don't even feel as if I own the things that are purportedly mine. I imagine you looking quizzically at me right now, as if to ask what could possibly account for such a kooky feeling. And I don't know how to explain it except to say that the survival of all your things in the wake of your death — you gone, they still here, vividly here — has led me to realize that our so-called possessions have an independence of sorts, a life of their own, a durability greater than ours that makes it preposterous to think we could ever own them. At most, I'm now inclined to believe that we coexist for awhile, that they pass through our hands, or we through theirs in the case of things like the house, which might outlast us both for hundreds of years. That being the case, it seems more accurate to think of myself as a steward rather than an owner, just looking after things, taking care of them awhile as best I can, hoping I might find them a good home before I shuffle off this mortal coil. Possession, after all, is only nine-tenths of the law.

THURSDAY, DECEMBER 19
Dear Kate,

Holly and I had lunch today to review how things are going with the nonfiction list that I'm editing for the press. She's such a thoughtful person and genial publisher that she didn't want to bother me with the details, though I figured they'd be a pleasant distraction. But before we got down to business, she asked me the usual question, with such a hopeful smile on her face that I didn't want to let her down. As if my continued anguish might be a breach of our friendship. Isn't it strange how we calibrate our feelings for the sake of our friends and colleagues? But it was so bad this morning that when I went out to put more straw on the garlic bed, a wave of grief swept over me at the thought of you not being here next July to harvest and braid it. When

I finished telling her about my outburst, she looked at me solemnly and said, "This is definitely going to take a whole year. Don't you think so?" To which I replied that I didn't think I'd ever get over it. "Oh yes, of course, of course," she agreed. Yet it was also clear that in some sense she imagined a year would be sufficient for me to get through the worst of it. And she's not the only one. This afternoon, on the way home from walking Puck, I met up with Bob and Margaret, who were just back from England, heard about your death, and had stopped at the house to leave a donation for the memorial fund. So of course they asked how I'm doing, and of course I didn't let on, but Bob advised me not to make any important decisions for a year, like selling the house, or moving to another part of the country. And I assured him that I plan to stay in the house until someone carries me out of it feet first. And that was that. Still, I couldn't help wondering about the repeated prognosis of a year to recover my emotional bearings. First it was Gene, then others, now Holly and Bob. So many people mouthing the same message that it must have an element of truth, though I wonder if it's anything more than saying that time heals all wounds. I mean, what's so magical about a year, which seems like a moment compared to the eternity of your absence. And if a year is the measure, does that mean I'm supposed to be feeling a little better every day, every week, every month? Not judging from my experience so far. And not according to Trudy, and she ought to know, given the death of her father and now of her mother. She told me that my recent plunge is the sort of thing that's likely to happen again, much as I'm likely to have periods of relative calm, without any why or wherefore. So, all I can do is take my pulse and give you a daily report. A year from now, if I'm still writing, perhaps I'll have something to say about the difference a year makes.

FRIDAY, DECEMBER 20

Dear Kate,

I've been crying so much the past two weeks that I'm on the verge of becoming a professional griever, capable of shedding a few tears on cue. How else to explain what happened this morning when I was doing some late Christmas shopping and bumped into Judy and Bob? She immediately told me how much she's been thinking about you, "still shocked" by your sudden death. Being your cancer nurse for so long, it's not surprising that she was curious about what happened, so I told her the story of that afternoon, which I've been trying not to think about or talk about the past few days. In the middle of the story, I could see her bright blue eyes turning red and beginning to moisten, and just then I felt as if my eyes should be keeping pace with hers, and sure enough I began to moisten up a bit myself. How's that for creepy behavior? I had turned on the tap just like that, like an actor, and it made me feel so crappy I decided then and there that I had to rein myself in, resist the impulse to cry so often, lest I become an emotional fraud, a theatrical widower — in other words, an object of pity and a sure cause for self-loathing. Firmly resolved, I went home to box up more presents for shipping, but didn't have anything large enough to hold them all, so I opened one of the mail-order packages that arrived for you a week or two after you died. (I've been storing them in our bedroom, not wanting to look at their contents.) No sooner did I pull up the flaps, pull out the packing, and see that it was filled with toys for the pets, traveling games for us, and other amusements than I started crying again, moaning about the cruel jest of your playful gifts. How's that for a Pagliacci-like bit of self-pity? And not even anyone around to behold my performance. But it was enough to make me feel so sleazy that I firmed up my earlier resolve, opened one of the toy mice, and let it loose on the kitchen floor for the amusement of Puck. And that did the trick — the big blue mouse so hectic with its spinning motion, its flashing green eyes, and its indecipherable French patter that I burst into laughter. Puck didn't find it quite so entertaining, especially when it suddenly stopped in midfloor, then just as quickly started spinning, flashing and chattering once again, then stopped and started, stopped and started again, until Puck was transfixed by its strange behavior — and I transfixed by Puck.

SATURDAY, DECEMBER 21

Dear Kate,

Early this morning, I dreamt of you again — dreamt of us, to be more exact, since you were lying on top of me, clothed in a t-shirt and green shorts. How's that for wish fulfillment? Better still, I had my hand under your shirt and was stroking your back, having undone your bra, and you asked, "What are you doing?" As if it weren't altogether obvious. Still, I felt you deserved the courtesy of an answer, so

I told you, "I'm stroking your back," by which time I was beginning to feel myself rise to the occasion, which evidently moved you to say, "Enough, enough, it's time to get up and get going." And sure enough I awoke, momentarily wondering what had provoked such a quaint dream, until I remembered having looked at several pictures of us when we were still courting, still discovering each other, some thirty-seven years ago, and you would ask me such delightfully prim questions and keep me at bay with such delightfully brisk evasions. Maybe I should keep looking at those pictures and showing them to others — who knows what dreams they might inspire!

Speaking of dreams, Martha called this morning to report that she saw you last night when you were much, much younger. "We were all up in the attic playing — Kate, Sarah, and me. Do you remember how big it was up there in the attic? Well, Kate and Sarah were at one end, and I was at the other. They were both wearing striped pinafores, laughing and playing together. Giggling a lot. And then they told me to look in the trunk that was at my end of the attic, but just when I opened the top and looked in they ran out of the room laughing, which made me call after them, 'Don't leave me alone! Why are you leaving me alone?'" At first, I thought her dream was about the childhood distance that must have separated her from you and Sarah, older by five and seven years, much as I felt such a childhood gulf between myself and my brother. But then I suddenly realized she was mourning the deaths of Sarah and you, mourning the fact of being virtually the only one left of your immediate family, and she's only in her fifties. Which made me realize as never before that she might be as grief-stricken as I — or even more. And that self-centered thought made me wonder whose grief is greater — hers or mine? But no sooner did I ponder that question than I remembered what you said on a similar occasion: "Don't be silly. It's absurd to think you can measure them against each other. Grief is grief, no matter who's feeling it or how they express it."

SUNDAY, DECEMBER 22

Dear Kate,

Today, on this day of rest, when you and I would ordinarily have lounged around the house, I was out and about from start to finish — having coffee, then lunch, then dinner, and with three different people.

Such a hectic change of pace that it made me think I'm as out of control as when we first met and I was dating so many women, a different one each night, that you took me in hand, lest I burn myself out in a Don Juanesque frenzy. "I'll be your friend," you said. "That's what you need to help get your life under control." Well, that's exactly what I need right now — someone or something to help get my life, or at least my schedule, in order. For today's not the only time I've overdone it. I'm just a guy who can't say no, so things pile up in unavoidable ways, like today, when I had a previously arranged dinner date, but then got a last-minute call inviting me to lunch, and then got an e-mail from my former student Marilyn, who wanted to touch base about her book before she leaves for the holidays. So much for the resolve I made on Friday not to have more than one outing a day. I wish it were a simple matter to say no, but I'm beginning to think there's more to it than that. Like having someone or something so important in one's life that it can't be frittered away in a whirl of social engagements. But with you gone, I've lost my spine, lost my sense of purpose, and don't know where to find them. Sometimes I think about getting back to my book on the personal essay, but I can't do it and these letters too. Yes, yes, I can imagine your rejoinder — "Don't use me as an excuse not to work on your book." If only I didn't have such an excuse.

MONDAY, DECEMBER 23

Dear Kate,

"Y'all ready for Christmas?" That's what the cashier asked me, flashing a big smile as I put my groceries on the checkout counter — a half gallon of Starbuck's lowfat latte ice cream to sweeten my imagination and a tube of Neosporin to heal my cracked lip. I wanted to tell her the truth, but I didn't want to rain on her parade, so I flashed a smile right back and said, "You bet!" — the words she was eager to hear. As for Christmas, I've not even been up to buying myself a small tree. A week or so after you died, I stopped at the market to eyeball some ten-footers, on the chance that I might hold our annual tree-trimming party. A foolish thought, of course, but I haven't forsaken the idea of a tree, thanks to the memory of that time in Hawaii when you made one out of driftwood. So, I've decided to decorate the pink-flowered geranium — it's now more than three feet tall — with a few ornaments. I got the idea a few nights ago when I was showing Holly and Lain some pictures from our trips to Hawaii, and came upon the shot of you all got up in your tropical pants suit, with a maile leaf lei around your neck, standing next to the potted driftwood, with a Hawaiian ornament in your hand, ready to decorate your "tree" and then to have dinner overlooking the ocean. In honor of that memory, I'm going to decorate my "tree" tonight at a party attended only by me, Jag, and Puck. Then perhaps I'll be ready for Christmas.

WEDNESDAY, DECEMBER 24

Dear Kate,

After dinner last night, I decorated my tree without any help from Jag, who was asleep in the attic, and without much interest from Puck, who viewed the proceedings from the living room couch. A solitary affair, but mildly pleasurable just the same, rummaging through your cache of ornaments, where I found the ear of golden corn with a green sheath, which fit perfectly on the upper right-hand side, and a bright red tomato that seemed to belong on the lower left. A couple of pleated ribbons went nicely in the upper part of the plant, the knitted bluebird of happiness mid-left, and the striped fish with a heart on its scales front and center. After eyeballing the decorated plant, I put my presents under it and called it an evening, content to have retrieved a little of the Christmas spirit — and a little of you too.

Speaking of contentment, I saw you again in a dream that seemed as if it was taking place this morning shortly after sunrise, when I was lying on my side in bed and you were nestled inside me. This time you didn't ask me what I was doing, but just smiled contentedly as I held you in my arms and then flashed a big smile when Puck came bounding up on the bed, from where I know not, since he'd ordinarily have been downstairs in his cage just then. It was a sweet, sweet dream all around, so vivid and tangible that it seemed as real as life itself, until I awoke with the shock of recognition. Five o'clock and the sky still dark. So I started reading Marilyn's manuscript, "The Men in My Country," a memoir of her time in Japan. And I thought of her prodigious loneliness and longing, which made me feel strangely blessed by you and the presence of all your handiwork. So I decided to share you (and the fruits of your labor) with a few people today.

First, a stop next door at Brad and Megan's with a jar of your currant-raspberry jam. Then a drive over to John's with a jar of your gingered lemon-lime marmalade and a bundle of photographs to show him what you looked like over the years. He was grateful, as usual, for the marmalade. But he really lit up when I showed him the modeling clips, especially the ones where you're posing amid a labyrinth of pipes in a refinery plant, garbed in a classically simple suit and a wide-brimmed hat. He also laughed at the one from the night before our wedding, where you're sitting in your mother's loveseat giving me the cold shoulder, and the one in our backyard, some ten years later, when we're facing each other, arms akimbo, in our red-checked shirts and cocky smiles — a standoff extraordinaire. By the end of my show, his eyes were aglitter — ocular proof you can still light up your admirers, even a nonagenarian beset by a brain tumor.

WEDNESDAY, DECEMBER 25

Dear Kate,

I wasn't looking forward to this morning, especially after an emotional breakdown last night, trying to drape the string of crimson stars on the living room banister, as you always did, with a dip, a rise, and another festive dip. Isn't it ridiculous how a little thing like that can make such a big difference? As if the world depended on a string of paper stars. But the sun rose and I arose, without being unstrung by your absence. Maybe I was so appalled at the prospect of a Kateless Christmas that the thing itself could never equal my fears. Or perhaps I've already been going through Christmas without you the past two weeks, and last night's breakdown was the climax. All passion spent, calm after the storm. Still, the prospect of opening presents alone, and nothing from you to open, seemed like such a downer that I delayed the business with a homemade waffle. And I thought about the time your mother gave us the old waffle iron that she'd gotten for a wedding present, with the spare announcement that "you can't make waffles for one." But I proved her wrong, thanks to the companionship of an article from the *New York Times*, "The Turtle Bay Area Immortalized by E. B. White." A piece about an aged willow that White once celebrated as a symbol of "life under difficulties, growth against odds." Fifty-four years having passed since White's tribute, the author of the *Times* piece wonders what might have come of the tree, especially given his anxieties about the durability of city life in the wake of 9/11. And he discovers that while its secondary branches have been cut away, the willow lives on, together with a sapling from one of its seeds. Such an emblem of endurance, such a commitment to perpetuating life, as you did in all your tree projects, that it left me shivering with delight. And so did a stupendous tree book from Trudy, wrapped in a flamboyant bow of gold ribbon that I wrapped around the newel post in place of the stars.

THURSDAY, DECEMBER 26

Dear Kate,

Here's a story from the department of haunting coincidences that begins at David and Rebecca's, where I went for Christmas dinner last night, and made the acquaintance of Rebecca's brother-in-law, who raved about your magical way with his learning-disabled students, telling me how you treated them as if they were regular schoolchildren and they performed better for you than ever before. I remember your talking about a school teacher and his students who came to help at the heritage grove, but never imagined meeting him at David and Rebecca's. A Christmas delight more heady than a flute of champagne, but nothing compared to what I heard after meeting Rebecca's sister, an emergency-room nurse who, believe it or not, was on duty there when you were brought in that afternoon. "She was still talking when they wheeled her in, but they knew she was going to die." Such dizzying news, so long after the fact, on so festive an occasion — we were standing in the living room, surrounded by a bevy of Rebecca's relatives — that I could hardly deal with it at first. You were still talking! It never occurred to me, given how far gone you were when I arrived. What were you saying, what had I missed? But she, alas, was only a bystander, not assigned to your case, so didn't hear the exact words, just that you were still talking. Your last words lost — that was all I could think of at first, and then how I should have come with you in the ambulance, and then how I should have done this and that, my mind racing until it was brought up short by the brunt of her other statement. How did they know you were going to die before they did a CT scan or anything else? How did they know so soon? Even before I arrived, even before the doctor put his arm around my shoulder and said, "She's had a very bad stroke, and it's going to be a very long recovery, if she survives." Even before the neurologist showed me the CT scans, a dot of blood in the first image, a huge pool of it three or four scans down. Then and now a swirl of confusion and questions until Rebecca's sister looked at me calmly and said, "They pulled her finger and she didn't pull back. It's a classic sign of a flooded brain, a ruptured spinal cord, the central nervous system completely gone." There wasn't much for either of us to say after that. She assured me that nothing could have been done to save you. And I assured her that I was assured. And then it was time for dinner and we passed the platters and filled our plates and filled our goblets and I drank enough to flood my brain with wine.

FRIDAY, DECEMBER 27
Dear Kate,

Today, for the first time since you died, I moved some of my clothes into the top drawer of your dresser, and then thought how strange it was that I'd taken so long to move in, seeing as how the dresser sits by my side of the bed and I've always coveted it. (Which reminds me of the Chinese maxim, to beware of asking lest your wish be granted.) Maybe it's taken so long because I'm so accustomed to your clothes being in our bedroom and mine in the guest bedroom. Only yesterday, for instance, did I move my winter shirts and t-shirts into your closet, but this morning I reflexively went looking for them in mine. Then again, I wonder if it isn't a deeply ingrained resistance to living without you, so deeply ingrained that I still refer to "your closet" and "my closet," "your dresser" and "my dresser."

Everything else in the house is almost the same as it was the day you died, except for the shots of you that I've displayed in the living room, and the bowls you bought just before you died that I've put on the sideboard in the dining room. Even your fall gourd display still sits on the dry sink in the dining room, and the black vase (with your ashes in it) still resides in its accustomed place in the corner of the living room. Oh yes, I can hear you saying, "Don't make a fetish of me," or words to that effect. But I'm not doing anything of the sort. Everything is so lovely just as you left it that I can hardly bear the thought of changing things, as I discovered in a dream early this morning. I was walking toward the house from downtown, and the minute it came into view, I was shocked to see the porch ripped away, the foundation gaping open, the front lawn heaved up and littered with sewer pipes, the side lawn covered with cement, and workers swarming everywhere, tearing things up so badly that I ran toward the back door, hoping you'd be in the kitchen, hoping you'd assure me it was all part of a grand remodeling plan. And sure enough you were there, standing by the cooktop, your back to the door, stirring something in your big copper pot. But when I called out your name and you turned around, it turned out that you were someone else completely, someone I had never seen before, her face so cruel, eyes and lips so full of scorn, that I suddenly awoke, shaking and dripping with sweat. Talk about nightmares! That's what it's like to be here without you.

SATURDAY, DECEMBER 28

Dear Kate,

I've just returned from a cemetery walk with Puck, the air so mild (in the 50s!) that it felt like mid October rather than late December, much as it did ten years ago this day, when you, I, and Pip took the very same walk with Hannah and Monty before their return to California. The mind, it seems, veers inexorably to the past, and there's no stopping its reflexive moves. Now, for example, I'm thinking of you even more than usual, and not just because I'm writing you this letter, but also because it's 4:40 P.M., Saturday, exactly five weeks from the moment you died. "Don't go there," you'd surely say. Besides, it's ridiculous to make more of this day than any other. As if anniversaries were measured in weeks rather than years, which makes me wonder if I'll soon be measuring in months rather than weeks, and so by degrees become accustomed to the years. Maybe that's how time heals — slowly, very slowly, like the growth of new bark around a severed oak limb.

Speaking of anniversaries, do you remember when we were in California last year for Thanksgiving, how we talked about a Thanksgiving get-together in Hawaii? A family reunion in Hanalei? Well, I've been thinking of that very thing for next November, the anniversary of your death. It all started when Amy called a few days ago about coming to visit me tomorrow, and she mentioned a surprising conversation that she had with you when the three of us were in Hanalei last March, and you told her that you'd be happy to have your ashes scattered there. Did you really say that? I could hardly believe it at first, given how often you bristled when I asked you to scatter my ashes there, as if you thought it sentimental and presumptuous of me to make such a request. So I asked her again, and she surprised me again with the news that you told her the same thing when we were there two years ago. But then I remembered your telling me just a few months ago that you considered Hawaii a source of spiritual renewal. Such a surprising announcement by the doyenne of the down-to-earth that I've decided to take you back to Hanalei one last time, scatter your ashes in the bay on the anniversary of your death, and give thanks for all our times there the past twenty years. When Hannah called yesterday, I told her about my plan, and she of course wanted to know, "Can Ben and Lizzie come too?" So she was delighted when I told her that you had wanted to have a real family reunion — children, grandchildren, and all. Amy, of course, has already signed on. I also plan to invite Martha, and I might ask Trudy too. A full house, a full table, thanksgiving by the sea.

SUNDAY, DECEMBER 29
Dear Kate,

Amy and Joe drove down from Wisconsin this afternoon for a short visit, so I spent much of the day on household chores, except for writing a thank-you note to Linda — such a devoted neighbor that the past month she's evidently been lighting candles for you almost every night at the park. I first noticed them a few days after you died but didn't want to go snooping around the neighborhood to find out who was doing it. Then a couple of days ago, when I was looking out the kitchen window, I finally saw her lighting them at sunset, and then saw her doing it again last night, with her dogs in tow. I should have known it was Linda — as gruff and tender as ever. So I wrote her a note and delivered it with a basket of your jams and jellies. "You shouldn't have done that," she said. "I'm enjoying it and plan to keep it going for a long time. Kate did so much for the neighborhood." But then she looked at the jars with your handwritten labels — "Currant Jelly,"

"June Jam," "Dark Cherry Preserves" — and said, "You mean she made all these herself? Every summer? I love that kind of stuff." So, you'll be sweetening her breakfasts for weeks to come.

After dinner this evening, I had a sweet conversation with Amy and Joe about you and the afternoon you died and the inexorable process of grieving. A surprising conversation, given my discovery of how deeply Joe's been touched by the death of his father and sister. So deeply that he of the Viking build and self-assured manner told me unashamedly that "you'll never get over it, never, I never have, but in time you'll learn to live with it as best you can, and the best way to do that is to play different movies in your mind — not of Kate dying in the ICU, but of you and Kate at your favorite place in Hawaii or Iowa City or just in your own backyard." Grief counseling from my son-in-law the science teacher, that sounds a bit like those stress-reduction tapes you brought home a few years ago, filled with the soothing vibes of birdsong and ocean waves. As in, "Go somewhere else." If only you were there when I arrived.

MONDAY, DECEMBER 30

Dear Kate,

Talk about a tear-jerker — today was it, beginning with a second Christmas, thanks to Amy and Joe bringing their presents to open them here — and a surprise package for me from you. Amy broke it to me gently: "Dad, Hannah and I found these things at the back of Kate's closet when we were clearing out her clothes last month, and we figured they were meant for you . . . for Christmas. So." She paused before handing me the package, and then of course I started to choke up. Yes, I know, it wasn't that much — a pebbled pair of gardening gloves, a travel pack of playing cards, a black enameled grill pan. But each one has the mark of your discriminating eye — the gloves with cutoff fingertips, the narrow cards in a small carrying case, the pan just right for you and me. Looking at those things, holding them in my hand — all of them just right for the hand — I hardly knew what to say, overwhelmed as I was by surprise, and then by the remembrance of you always working on Christmas even before Thanksgiving was done, always getting things I needed or wanted, without even asking. But the pain of remembering was nothing compared to those visible embodiments of your intention broken in midstride, which put me in mind of the cloth you bought in Kauai for your reversible bathrobe, all cut and ready to be sewn, and your notebooks filled with draft poems waiting to be revised, and the tree-survey reports yet to be collated and analyzed. "One mind less, one world less."

After the presents, our talk turned to plans for your memorial service in late May and then the fall trip to Hanalei — a farewell not only to you but also to Hawaii, since I can't imagine myself ever going back without you. And then, as if to change the subject, Amy wanted to meet Sarah — one intensive-care nurse to another — so it was off to the hospital for a brief conversation that led her to assure me on the way home, "It couldn't have been any better, Dad, given a nurse of her own like Sarah. The outcome was bound to be disastrous — it couldn't have been any different with a bleed that big — but at least she got excellent care. It couldn't have been any better. I could see that just from talking to Sarah." I couldn't disagree, but I couldn't help noticing the irrepressible impulse to look for consolation in the midst of disaster. And not just in Amy, but in me too. Why else would I have told her and Joe it was a miracle of sorts that the stroke didn't hit just a few minutes earlier while you were driving home from the fair, otherwise you might also have had a horrific accident. Nothing like an even more grievous possibility to lessen one's grief. A bottle of champagne in late afternoon also helped take the edge off things, as did a sumptuous meal at Adagio and memories of our dinner there the night before you died.

TUESDAY, DECEMBER 31

Dear Kate,

Here it is, last day of the year, and it began as if it might be the last day of my life, when I woke at two thirty this morning, face flushed, hands moist, stomach bloated and aching. I lay on my side a few minutes, until it dawned on me that I might be having a heart attack. Then fumbled to take my pulse, but it was racing so fast I couldn't count the beats. Tachycardia! Only then did I begin to take stock of everything I had to drink and eat last night — three glasses of champagne at home before going to dinner, where I had two glasses of wine, together with an appetizer of sautéed scallops, the creamy wine sauce sopped up with bread, followed by salad with a dense balsamic vinaigrette, then a richly sauced chicken breast served over a bed of arborio rice, and to top it all off, a large slice of chocolate mousse, a bit of which I shared with Amy and Joe. "Wouldn't it be something," I thought, "to die of a heart attack just a few weeks after Kate's demise. Everyone will think I died of a broken heart, when the truth is that I was done in by my appetite." And then, of course, I remembered how upset you got whenever I overdid it, especially after that episode here at home when you took me to the emergency room and it turned out to be nothing more than a gastrointestinal overdose. "From now on, you're on your own," you announced, "and don't wake me up the next time," but you always woke up without my nudging you. Without you, I had no choice but to try the bathroom and hope that a bowel movement, aspirin, and deep breathing would do the trick. No such luck — heart still racing, hands still moist, cheeks still flushed, I stumbled into the guest room and woke Amy, figuring that she, the intensive-care nurse, would surely be able to tell whether I should call 911 or just wait for the symptoms to pass. And sure enough, she took my pulse several times, noticed it gradually subside, along with the end of my sweating palms, which led her to surmise that it was probably just another gastrointestinal episode. But then she strongly advised me to call 911 if I ever have such an episode again. "Don't wait, Dad, 'cause time is tissue, and you never know whether it's the real thing."

Speaking of real things, I made a sociological discovery today — namely that New Year's Eve day is evidently a time for the consolation of grieving widowers. How else to account for a day of long-distance calls and out-of-town visitors? The most memorable was Judith, back in town for a few days and couldn't resist a visit to her old neighborhood. She turned up in the driveway, just when Amy and Joe were leaving, and almost unstrung me by the way she talked about you in that flat no-nonsense voice of hers — "She was amazing, one of the most amazing people I've ever known. She told me once she was 'just a recluse poet.' But all the while I knew she was taking care of the neighborhood park and Heritage Trees. And without looking for any attention, just doing it. How did she do it all, and still have time to make her own clothes? I mean, when did she get up in the morning? I'll bet she never wasted her time on TV." But when I told her about you reading in bed every morning and watching television every night, her eyes widened and again she exclaimed, "Amazing. Amazing. You were a very, very lucky man!" Of course I agreed, wishing to myself that you had been a luckier woman. No sooner had Judith left with your yellow silk scarf in hand than I got a call from my cousin Natalie, wondering what I had planned for New Year's Eve, and I told her how we always had oysters, champagne, and your citrus-pomegranate salad with champagne vinaigrette, but this year instead I was having dinner with Marybeth and Ken. Given this morning's gastrointestinal episode, I didn't miss the oysters. But then again, perhaps we could have had something different, you and I — you in your new Hawaiian bathrobe, I in an old aloha shirt.

WEDNESDAY, JANUARY 1
Dear Kate,

From the pickled artichokes to the roast pork tenderloin, dinner last night with Marybeth and Ken was a wine-drenched feast. But most of the time, I was so envious of Ken that I could hardly enjoy the food. It's not that I covet his wine cellar or Marybeth, though God knows she's lovely in more ways than one — and so is his wine. No, it's the simple fact of her being alive (and you dead) that made me jealous, especially after her heart problem this summer and fall. So weak at times you worried about her survival, especially after she overdid it working on the old schoolhouse. Last night, she looked so attractive I could hardly take my eyes off her, even with Ken at the dinner table. Thanks to the seating arrangement, I could gaze at her without turning my head, without being noticed. But I felt like an imposter, especially when the conversation turned to memories of you and the usual question of how I've been doing. I wonder what they'd have said if I told them how I was doing just then. It's not the first time I've had such creepy feelings — in fact, the same thing has happened with our other married friends, which makes me wonder if it's like this with other widowers, for if that's the case I don't know how often I'm up to such outings. But now at least I can sympathize with an essay by Lamb that I was reading just a few days before you died — "A Bachelor's Complaint on the Behaviour of Married Couples." Literature and life — the connection holds true even in a two-hundred-year-old essay by an eccentric bookkeeper.

Too bad he didn't have any light to shed on my bill-paying today. But nothing he wrote could have cushioned me from the renewal notice for your membership in the Dramatists Guild and my memory of how proud you were when you learned that the staged reading of your *Cassandra* made you eligible to join. And it wasn't any better with the list of charges for your afternoon in the hospital. No sooner had I finished scanning it than the words came rushing out of my mouth, "Dying, Kate, is more costly than you might imagine — more than seven thousand dollars for just a few hours of care. Such a pricey thing, Kate, you'd never approve. But believe it or not, we only had to pay eight hundred dollars, thanks to Blue Cross Blue Shield. Just eight hundred dollars to shuffle off your mortal coil in grand style." Such a melodramatic outburst that Puck came in from the living room, sat on his haunches, and stared at me with an intense look of concern. And I in turn was so embarrassed by his distress that I shut off the faucet, did the rest of the bills in silence, and then took refuge in the bowl games. Some New Year's.

THURSDAY, JANUARY 2

Dear Kate,

You'd probably have said, "Don't go there," if I had asked you about watching *South Pacific* last night on TV. But I was bent on seeing Hanalei again, given my plan to scatter your ashes there in November. The only problem is that I tuned in just when Rossano Brazzi was starting to sing "Some Enchanted Evening," with the moonlit bay visible in the background. And the words that followed, "You may see a stranger across a crowded room," reminded me of the first time I saw you across a crowded room some thirty-seven years ago, so dazzled that all I could do was stand there and stare, too shy to introduce myself. After hearing that song and remembering that time in our lives, I should have switched channels then and there. But I kept on watching and weeping, like a bingeing nostalgiaholic, until I was so disgusted with myself that I turned it off after the Bali Ha'i episode, took Puck out for a brisk walk in the cold night air, and remembered the miracle that brought us together, when I walked into the department office one day just as Rosie was pasting your ID picture on your student folder. Talk about romantic destiny! Maybe that's why the movie got to me last night. Now I wonder what you were thinking all those nights you watched it on TV.

After the movie, I was so filled with yearning that I went to bed hoping to see you in my dreams, wondering, in fact, if I could will myself to dream of you. "I want to dream of Kate," said I to myself. "Let's dream about her, let's think about dreaming about her, and see what happens." What happened is that I woke up at a quarter to six without having dreamt about you or anything else. But a short essay about snake rustlers and snake fanciers in southwest Texas was just what I needed, for it left me tired enough to fall back asleep and dream of you just before I awoke. You were standing by the cooktop, and I was sitting just a foot or two away at the kitchen table, listening to you talk about a woman you've never mentioned, a woman who grew up in your hometown of Lisbon, but now lives in southwest Texas. (Isn't it fascinating how the mind takes bits and pieces from our waking life and weaves them into our dreams?) Anyhow, your recollections of that woman were so animated, your eyes and voice so lively, that I found myself looking up at you in wonderment and admiration, and you in turn seemed a bit larger than life as you became more involved in your recollections, and as the melody from "Some Enchanted Evening" started rising in the background, until I was so carried away by you and your voice and the music and my desire that I rose from my chair and hugged you, and hugged you, in a buzz of delight. And then, of course, I awoke, dazed and dizzy, but also deeply touched by the gradual awareness that the movie had given me the dream of my desires.

So, perhaps, there's no telling what might come of all this grief. Maybe like last night, the memories of you which now cause me pain will gradually become a form of solace. That's what Trudy and Hannah have been telling me these days. Still, I'm haunted by the way that things can suddenly bring you to mind, like yesterday's bout with the monthly bills. When I told that to Caroline, who called this afternoon, she did a riff on grief that's still ringing in my ears: "There's no safety in writing checks," she said. "There's no safety anywhere. That's what I discovered when my mother died. So all you can do is watch out for booby traps, they're everywhere, even when you're just watching ads on TV. If they remind you of something, they remind you of something."

SUNDAY, JANUARY 5,

Dear Kate,

By this time, I'm sure, you'd be telling me to pull up my socks and get on with it. So, this morning, right after putting Puck out for his morning constitutional, I put all your African violets into the kitchen sink to bottom-water them, before going back upstairs to shower and shave. Then in preparation for Trudy's visit later this week, I stripped the sheets off the guest bed and took them down to the washing machine, before bringing Puck back in for his breakfast and mine. After an omelet and a bit of the *New York Times* (our Sunday tradition continues), I was back into chore mode, moving the sheets from the washer to the dryer and choking up a bit at the sight of all your Christmas wrappings, your boxes of Heritage Trees brochures, your amaryllis planter waiting to be replenished with new potting soil, your fruit room fully stocked from this summer's canning and the summers past. Back upstairs again to make Trudy's bed, I was suddenly visited by a Martha Stewartish idea — to use two different-colored sheets rather than one matching set. So I put a blue sheet over the mattress and topped it with a yellow sheet and yellow pillowcases, which go very cheerfully with the blue flower-basket quilt. No wonder you dubbed me Carlita. Beholding the blue and yellow bedding, I suddenly felt a momentary rush of satisfaction that housewives, I gather, used to thrive on (and maybe still do), and then in my mind's ear I also heard you wryly deflating my little balloon with that sixties' mantra of yours, "Whatever turns you on!" With that advice in mind, I returned to the kitchen to see what we need from the grocery store, when I heard you once again, "Make a list, make a list, or you'll make a mistake and forget something." So I pulled out one of your three-by-five cards and made a complete list, with marginal notations of where to shop for each — "C" for the co-op, "E" for the Eagle, and "H" for Hy-Vee. Those marginal abbreviations were such a new wrinkle that I was again feeling a Martha Stewartish frisson of delight, quickly stifled again by your mantra, "Whatever turns you on!" So after finishing my list, I went upstairs to make our bed, when I heard you one more time, "Wouldn't you like to try a different set? Don't forget, change is of the essence." So I folded up the newly washed sheets, remembering how much easier it was to fold them when you were on the other end and we could snap out the wrinkles together. Then I put on a different set, remembering how much easier it was to make the bed when you were on the other side and we could smooth out the wrinkles together. And then back downstairs to put Puck in his cage, before heading off to the store, which I won't tell you about in detail, since the point of this story is already so clear that it needs no more telling. You've trained me so well, I can carry on alone, but it's not quite as easy without you, and it's not what turns me on, not without you.

MONDAY, JANUARY 6

Dear Kate,

Dining out last night with Caroline and Len, I was surprised to find myself telling humorous stories about my tachycardic episodes and reveling in their laughter. Gallows humor? Comic distraction? Grief intolerable except by deflection? Or too much wine before dinner? Whatever the cause, I'm puzzled by my behavior, so completely different from when I'm alone. In fact, I can't remember such a joyous moment since the night before you died, when you and Gene and I were catching up over drinks at Adagio. Everyone tells me not to worry about having a good time now and then, but I wonder what you'd say on this score. Would you tell me, as you often did, that "guilt is not a useful reaction, it's just a neurotic form of self-indulgence"; or would you reprove me for spending so much time with others, when we had so little time for ourselves; or would you say in that inscrutable way of yours, "Whatever turns you on"? As you can see, I'm looking for guidance, and there aren't any clear-cut answers, except for the one you gave me just a few weeks before you died when I was picking your brain about something — "You can't keep relying on me," you said, "to figure things out. Someday I'm not going to be here, and then what?"

Speaking of which, I can tell you I'm still going through all the routines we devised to keep the animals apart — Puck leashed on the back porch, Jag asleep upstairs, or Puck in the attic with me while Jag roams the backyard, or both of them in the house on different floors, separated by the barrier. As if I were the master of ceremonies in a bedroom farce, but without your deft assistance. And thereby hangs a tale (no pun intended). This afternoon, when I was in the kitchen, Jag leapt over the barrier from the upstairs to the downstairs, Puck attacked him on the living room floor, Jag hissing all the while in full threat-display, and I completely lost it. You'd have loved my melodramatic wail at Puck — "Don't you realize what's up, that she's gone, she's gone, and she's not coming back, not coming back ever again? So we have to get along with each other, we have to, and if you can't lay off of Jag, then I'll have to take you away, find you another home, 'cause I can't deal with this stuff alone." Then, believe it or not, he backed off, tail down, and stared at me in distress — such a remorseful look in his eyes that I felt like an abusive master.

TUESDAY, JANUARY 7

Dear Kate,

At the supermarket this morning, I was outraged by the sight of an elderly woman — scraggly hair, pasty complexion, puffy cheeks — as ill-kempt as her faded cotton dress, bulging at the seams, tattered at the hem. Down and out in Iowa City, spending what little she had on a six-pack of beer. A pathetic figure, more deserving of sympathy than rage. But all I could think of just then was her alive and you dead, despite your careful regimen and your good works. No wonder your mother could hardly make sense of things after your father died, seeking answers in self-help books, as if anything could explain the outrageousness of his sudden death. Even younger, and healthier it seemed, than you. Such a monstrous injustice that she couldn't stop reading *When Bad Things Happen to Good People*. It never occurred to me that she might also be angered by the spectacle of good things happening to bad people, not until I read about a notorious gangster recovering from a brain hemorrhage like yours. But that was nothing compared to how I sometimes feel just at the sight of an elderly couple hand in hand, blithely taking a stroll in the park or window-shopping downtown, as if they hardly realize their extraordinary good fortune. Why should they have it and you not? That's what drives me crazy sometimes, and surely must have gotten to your mother, especially in that small town with all her married friends nearby. Now, now all too late, I wish we'd asked her how she dealt with the envy and the anger, but it seemed like such a private matter, except for that ever-present book on her coffee table, that I never wanted to intrude. So I'm left to my own devices, and depending on the day or my mood, the remedies vary. Sometimes all it takes is a reality check like this — "But surely you wouldn't wish those others dead, even if it would bring her back alive!" And sometimes it's the realization that you had a longer life than many others, especially given those fifteen years after your first bout with cancer. And sometimes it's the awareness of how intensely you lived before the letting go. So many rationalizations it's no wonder you sometimes called me Pollyanna or Doctor Pangloss — as if I could possibly think that "all's for the best in this best of all possible worlds."

FRIDAY, JANUARY 10

Dear Kate,

My barber, whom I haven't seen since you died, was so touched by the news that he wouldn't let me pay for my haircut this morning, but shook my hand as I left and asked me to contribute the money to your memorial fund. He clearly knew what I've been going through, given what he said about the sudden death of his sister-in-law last July, and the anguish that it's caused him as well as his brother. Talking to people who've experienced such a loss and then to others who haven't, I've come to realize the enormous gulf that divides the haves from the have-nots. To know firsthand the fragility and unpredictability of life is what makes all the difference — and to live without such knowledge is to exist, I now think, in an extraordinary state of ignorance, unless one happens to be endowed with your uncanny sense of foreboding. Though I don't have your prescience and never will, I've recently had a premonition that I might be carried off as suddenly as you a month or so from now. No, I'm not competing — just remembering how it was a few years ago when you broke your right ankle shortly after Thanksgiving, and then the very day you finished your rehab, I broke my right ankle too, which led folks to joke about us being so closely bonded that we even coordinated our injuries. So you can see why I might imagine myself being carried off any day now as suddenly as you — also why I've been more concerned than usual to put our affairs in order as soon as possible.

Yesterday, for example, I called Schwab to send me change-of-beneficiary forms for my retirement accounts, and today I called Nancy to arrange for the Jones house in Hanalei next November. Though she's no longer managing rentals along the bay, she's still overseeing the Jones house and living in the caretaker's cottage again, and she sounds as buoyant as ever. But the news of your death shocked her so much that she momentarily sounded like a stuck record, muttering "I can't believe it," again and again. The minute she got back on track, though, Nancy was Nancy again, not only assuring me that the house will be available but also offering to arrange for an outrigger canoe crew to take us into the bay, so we can scatter your ashes in a traditional Hawaiian manner. Then I called Amy and Hannah to tell them about the arrangments. So if I happen to be carried away before then, they can scatter my ashes there along with yours, and we can haunt the bay together, just as we walked the beach in years gone by.

SATURDAY, JANUARY 11
Dear Kate,

Bitterly cold weather returned last night, as well as more thoughts about being on the beach or anywhere else but here. So I called Martha this afternoon and accepted her invitation to Largo. I remember you had talked about our going there sometime in the next year or two. The past several weeks, in fact, I gradually got the idea of doing a tour of Florida, especially since Gene invited me down to his place in Key West, and then Lynda called from Chicago asking me to visit her and Ron at a house they've rented in Sarasota. Such loyal friends that I could hardly refuse, but I'm a bit uneasy about traveling without you, especially after the loneliness of my trip to Quebec last summer, but I need to get out of here and away from the animals for awhile. In other words, a warm respite from the cold weather, a chance to stretch out a bit with friends and relatives, and a solo flight to see how I do on my own. I've heard about people traveling to get away from reminders of their grief, but that's certainly not in the cards with a trip to see Martha and Gene. Come to think of it, I can't imagine two other people more certain to remind me of you and your demise. Still, I also can't imagine an easier place to go right now for a midwinter break.

SUNDAY, JANUARY 12
Dear Kate,

When I was out walking Puck last night, I couldn't stop thinking about a conversation I had with Jon and Pamela, who stopped over to see me yesterday afternoon. Though he's settled again in Chicago, writing a regular column for the *Tribune*, he's still so hooked on Iowa City from his graduate-student days in the nonfiction program that he keeps coming back like a homing pigeon. We were sitting around the dining room table, sipping tea, talking about this and that — Pamela's newly finished movie, Jon's new book project, my letters to you, and each of our bouts with the death of loved ones. I knew, of course, how hard it had been when his son died a few years ago, but I hadn't known that Pamela has lost both of her parents in the past two years. Their grief, in other words, is still very green. Yet they talk of it so knowingly and articulately that I found myself hanging on their words, hungry for whatever guidance they might offer. ("When does the grief end?" I keep wondering to myself.) So you can imagine how fascinated I was when Jon told me that he came to terms with his loss through an act of faith — through what appeared to be a traditional Christian belief in life after death, and thus, in the continued existence of his son, whom he expects to meet when he himself passes on. A beautiful idea that I wish it were possible for me to believe. But given my longstanding skepticism and my intense sense of your absence, I couldn't hold back the words that came to me just then — in fact, I almost blurted them out: "She's not out there anywhere, not so far as I'm concerned, and that for me is the worst part of it all, not anywhere. I mean, I wish it were possible for me to believe in what you say, but I don't, and I haven't believed in such things for a long, long time." Jon was so upset by my remarks that his cheeks turned red as he came back at me: "But she is there in your memory, isn't she? And she's there in the memories of all the people who've written you those cards and letters, so many that they're overflowing that bowl in the living room. She touched many lives, just as you have, and you can't deny that she'll live on in their memories." I couldn't deny what he said, but I also felt compelled to point out the difference between living in the memory of others and being somewhere in the ions or in the great beyond. I was thinking just then of how it felt when I was six years old, newly orphaned by the death of my mother after my father had died a few years earlier, and how I sometimes imagined she was out there somewhere, "watching over me, looking out for me," as I used to think. In fact, I remember how I would sometimes lie on my back in the summer grass and look up intently into the passing clouds, confident that I would eventually see her up there somewhere if I lay there long enough, see an image of her in the clouds or maybe in the sky itself. But that, as they say, was in another country. Now I'm overwhelmed not just by your absence, but by my inability to believe in our ever meeting again, except in my dreams, my memories, and these letters I keep writing if only to make believe I can invoke you and speak to you whether you hear me or not.

MONDAY, JANUARY 13

Dear Kate,

In a dream last night, I was standing at the foot of the living room stairs, Amy beside me, the two of us trying to maneuver a long white plastic container down the stairway and into the living room. As the dream unfolded, you came into view at the top of the stairway, looked out over the second-floor railing, and told us exactly how to lift the container to get it off the stairs and into the living room. No sooner had we gotten it down than you reappeared with other containers and directions about where to store them. Just then the dream dissolved, and I awoke, momentarily dazed, then amused and fascinated by the image of those white plastic containers. Amused, because they look so much like the white plastic tank that I fill every night for the upstairs humidifier. Usually, I carry it downstairs and fill it at the kitchen sink, where I can rest it on the counter while it fills with water. But last night I didn't feel like going downstairs, so I tried to balance it single-handedly under the spigot in the bathroom tub — a difficult feat when it's filling with water. The sort of thing that put you out whenever I tried to cut corners around the house — "Do it right or don't do it at all," as you always said. But on a symbolic level that long rectangular container is shaped all too much like a coffin, an emblem of your death. And Amy is involved, I assume, because she's helped me to deal with some of the hardest and most painful questions about your death, from the moment I called her right after your stroke, to her visit after Christmas, when she put me at ease about the care you received at the hospital. But ultimately, I think, the image of you directing things at the top of the stairs is telling me that you above all others will be the one to guide me in the days and years to come. In the memory of your strength and wisdom, I will find the source of mine.

TUESDAY, JANUARY 14

Dear Kate,

That image of you at the top of the stairs was so vivid, but also so brief, that I sometimes find myself wishing we hadn't been scornful of home movies and videotapes, ever confident that we could see things better in our mind's eye. But now, now I'm not so sure, or perhaps it's just that I'm having a weak moment, and all I need do is tug a bit more at my memory or revisit my journals, where I can find you again and again — at book length. Besides, you probably wouldn't have let me tape you anyway ("Too artificial!"), especially given your increasing reluctance even to be photographed.

On the other hand, I'm sure you wouldn't object to the remedy suggested by a doctor who contacted me two or three years back after reading my retirement book. He e-mailed me again today, wanting to know how things are going for us, now that it's been a few years since the book appeared, so I had no choice but to tell him about your death and these letters. And he wrote back suggesting that I read *Gracie*, the memoir that George Burns wrote after his wife died, for it evidently contains some touching bits of wisdom, like the way he solved the problem of waking up at night and missing her — by moving over to her side of the bed. You always moved over to my side to do your morning reading, so why shouldn't I move over to yours to do my evening sleeping?

THURSDAY, JANUARY 16

Dear Kate,

Chris showed up this afternoon to do the yardwork that you asked him to take care of shortly before you died. I thought you had just wanted him to get rid of the volunteer brush and trim the lilacs, but the first thing he headed for was the big juniper. "I'm just sizing things up," he said, "before making the first cuts." He was crouching on the ground, so I crouched down beside him and told him that I hadn't expected anything to be done to the juniper. That's when he (and you) took me completely by surprise. "But that's what Kate asked me to do. She wanted me to cut it back, take down the overgrowth, get it under control." Talk about the force of your will — that's when I felt it more

strongly than any other time since you died, especially because I remembered your complaining about the juniper the last several years —
"It's blocking the gazebo, it's shading out my clematis, it's taking over
the hillock." You had so many things against it I'm surprised you didn't
take it down yourself, especially because you never shared my worry of
how naked the gazebo would look without the juniper. So I asked him
if he really thought it needed to be trimmed back, and he answered me
so quickly, so bluntly that I was taken by surprise — "If it was my
bush, I'd sure want to do something about all that overgrowth. It's out
of control." And again I felt the force of your will, even though it was
clear that he was giving me his own opinion. From that point on, I
could hardly oppose him — "What I plan to do is work from the bottom up, take off these lower limbs to begin with, to expose more of the
trunk, so it comes out looking like a bonsai." In fact, the minute he
started outlining his plan, I remembered that weekend some fifteen
years ago when you and I had a go-around with the bush — I resisting
your desire to cut it back, just as I did today, but then giving in when
you convinced me that we could make it look like a splendid bonsai
offsetting the gazebo. And we did — in fact, the more we took off the
better it looked, so much so that at one point you had to rein me in lest
I cut it back too much, which is just what happened today when Chris
was working on the south side of the bush, and I suggested that he cut
back some of the branches more severely than he planned. "It's easier
to take it off," he said, "than to put it back," which reminded me of
Merwin's "Unchopping a Tree," which reminded me of what it's been
like ever since you've gone and I've been trying to bring you back in
every way I know. It never occured to me that a bonsaied juniper could
do the trick. But today for just a moment, when I beheld the finished
thing, it felt as if you were there again, standing beside me, admiring
the work of our hands.

FRIDAY, JANUARY 17
Dear Kate,

There's a woman in the house, and it's not you, and it feels a bit
strange. It's Trudy, so I shouldn't be feeling this way, seeing as how
she's almost like family, and the guest room has always felt a bit as if it
were her bedroom. Still, I started to feel uneasy even before she ar-

rived, when I got the flowers for her dressing table yesterday morning. That's what you always did, so it seemed I should do the same thing. But when I brought the flowers home and started to arrange them — white tulips in the dark blue vase, red alstroemeria and larkspur in the blood red vase — it felt as if I were setting things up for a weekend tryst rather than a companionable visit. And it was exactly the same when I went to pick her up at the airport. Which makes me wonder what she's been thinking, especially because she sometimes seems a bit skittish about this and that — the dishes, the cooking, the schedule, our writing and where each of us should do it. Oh yes, she was delighted by the flowers, because they reminded her of you, and how you always put together a special bouquet for her dressing table. But sometimes she seems a bit uneasy, uncertain of herself. Maybe it's just because that's her way, or because she's being sensitive to my routines, not wanting to upset my applecart, and maybe that's what's going on with me, not wanting her to feel uneasy, especially given the fact that she too is in mourning. But then again, maybe we're both a bit ill at ease, because we're both missing the firm hand of your presence.

SATURDAY, JANUARY 18

Dear Kate,

It's just eight weeks since you died, but it often seems like many moons ago. I'm thinking in terms of moons, because the full moon is upon us — so bright it woke me three times last night, putting me in mind of that old favorite, "Full Moon and Empty Arms." Such a yearning melody, Rachmaninoff for the common man, that I could hear it running through my mind again, as it did when I was a lovesick high school student. Such an unbearable sense of longing that I tried to forget the melody and all its painful associations by turning to the *New Yorker*. The only problem is that I was immediately fascinated by a piece about recent attempts to elicit responses from the brains of people who are fully "locked in" — people, that is, who are so paralyzed that they can't even move their eyes or eyelids to express themselves. So paralyzed that their minds are completely locked in. I couldn't help wondering just then whether you were locked in during those last few hours in the hospital, whether you could hear me talking to you, whether you could feel me touching you, whether you yearned to express something in return, or whether you were so far away, so far gone that you couldn't hear anything or feel anything, much less desire to express anything. A profound conundrum that put me in mind again of that ironic little poem you wrote a few weeks before you died, about walking the walk alone.

I showed it to Trudy this morning, along with "Obit" and several others that you evidently wrote the last few months of your life, poems about death and dying — in your family, in the neighborhood, in your own imagined experience. And so many others on death and dying from years past that it made me think mortality might well have been the supreme theme of your art and song. No wonder you were so drawn to *Endgame* and *Krapp's Last Tape*. No wonder, too, that you readily agreed to do a modernized version of *Everyman* for the drama anthology. And yet I couldn't help noticing that your late-night writings are also filled with recipes from the TV food channel — a poem, a recipe, a poem, a recipe. Such a striking alternation between the world of food and the world of loss that it seems as if you must have been moving forever between them. At one moment in the here and now, and then wherever you happen to be now that you're no longer here.

SUNDAY, JANUARY 19

Dear Kate,

A few days ago, I was invited to serve on the board for Friends of Historic Preservation, and I agreed, seeing as how I know something about it from years of watching you do it. I also thought it would be a good way for me to get out of the house and do something more constructive than tending my grief. So this afternoon I went to the annual meeting of the group, but the minute I arrived so many people approached me, eager to say how sorry they were about your death, that I half wished I'd never agreed to serve (or attend today's meeting). I'm sure they were all sincere, but I still don't know what to say in response: "I'm sorry too"? "And so is she"? "We're both more sorry than you can imagine"? Sarcasm aside, the thing that really gets me when people talk that way is that I feel as if there's something visibly wrong with me. I felt somewhat like that when I was an orphan and my elementary-school playmates would ask about my father and mother. No harm intended, but I always felt embarrassed to say that my parents were dead, that I lived with my aunt and uncle, as if I were somehow deficient. And in a very real sense I was, just as I am yet again. As in, sometimes I feel like a motherless child.

MONDAY, JANUARY 20

Dear Kate,

Jix and Jean gave a dinner party last night — all of us longtime colleagues. A lovely gathering, but I couldn't help wondering what some of them were thinking about my arrival with Trudy in tow, especially given how striking she looked, with her silvery hair and her all-black outfit — "Not even two months gone, and here he is with a woman in hand!" Well, we weren't really hand in hand, but we did come together, and I didn't hide the fact that she was visiting me for several days, so there's no telling what thoughts might have been running through their heads. Carol, of course, knows Trudy from visits past, as does Jix from her postgraduate days in the institute for directors of writing programs. But who knows what the others might have been thinking? And who cares? And why should I be so ungenerous as to imagine my longtime colleagues even entertaining such thoughts? How strange to find myself as ill at ease as if I were a young instructor among strangers rather than a retired professor among friends. But then again, perhaps I'd feel more assured if you were by my side. Still, the evening as a whole was a pleasure, especially to see Trudy's eyes light up when she saw the cantilevered glass cabinets you designed for Jean and Jix in the manner of Frank Lloyd Wright, and to hear Jix report the admiration of folks from Taliesin when they saw your designs.

TUESDAY, JANUARY 21

Dear Kate,

This morning at Prairie Lights I introduced Trudy to Marilyn, who's back from the holidays, teaching again and working on her book for my nonfiction series. Though the drift of their lives has been different in many, many ways, it was fascinating to hear them ruminate on the pleasures of reclusiveness, on their desire to be alone for long periods of time. Which prompted Marilyn to ask how I've adjusted to being alone, which made me think of you and how reclusive you were when we first met — so devoted to your writing that you hadn't seen anyone or talked to anyone for four days before we got together. But you were never at a loss for words in your poems and plays, which has often made me wonder what might have come of your work had I not sought your affections, had I left you to your own devices. Would you have become a well-known poet or a widely produced dramatist, or would you have been distracted by the burdens of an academic job or by a marriage and children of your own? The road not taken and therefore a journey into mere conjecture. Still, I can't help thinking it was naive of me (and you) to suppose that marriage would not throw a wrench into your writing, especially given the intensity of your familial attachments. But I didn't share any of those troubling thoughts with Marilyn. I told her instead of how torn I am between the anguish of living without you and the solace of being alone to think of you and write you these letters. Letters I'd never be writing if you were still alive and we were still together. Which makes me wonder once again what might have come of you and your work had we never come together.

THURSDAY, JANUARY 23

Dear Kate,

Trudy and I put on a little dinner party last night, complete with candles, flowers, linen napkins, and a fully articulated menu, and the result evidently was such a touching embodiment of your spirit that midway through dinner David suddenly stood up saying, "Here's to Kate, here's to Kate," and everyone joined in, glasses on high to you. That's probably why I dreamt of you again this morning, though I was so hung over that everything's a bit blurry, except for the memory of our looking at each other nose to nose, between kisses and other tasty things, when suddenly you had to leave, and the last I saw of you was the back of your white shirt. Such a blatant ending that it needs no explanation.

But the most important news of the day is that Trudy's week-long visit has ended. Saying goodbye was hard for both of us — misery does, indeed, love company. But she's coming again for your memorial service this spring, as well as to Hawaii, so it's not as if we were parting forever. Just before leaving, she went into the living room and stared at the photos of you for several minutes on end, as if she wanted to fix them in her mind's eye or to commune with you from afar, then into the dining room to gaze at the shot of you walking into the distance along the Na Pali coast. "Would it be too much," she asked, "to have you make a copy of this for me?"

After Trudy boarded her plane, I met up with Raeburn, who sent me one of the most intensely compassionate letters I received. And again this afternoon he said something that really sticks in my mind. "No one, no one, can really know or feel what you're going through, no matter what they say, unless they've gone through something exactly like it." That's what I keep thinking to myself, though I don't say so publicly lest I offend those who tell me, "I know exactly how you feel." It's a strange thing how that innocent, well-meant remark can sometimes make me want to rise up and say, "No, you don't, no, you don't at all." But I keep my peace, knowing you'd have kept yours too.

FRIDAY, JANUARY 24

Dear Kate,

Here are a couple of episodes from "The Perils of Carl," which began last night just after I got home from dining out and discovered that the downstairs bathroom sink was nearly full, thanks to a dripping faucet, a frozen drainpipe, and the frigid crawlspace below. So I bailed out the sink, dumped the water into the toilet, and ran the hot water, in hope of unfreezing the drain. But no luck. Then, as a last recourse, I opened the doors of the cabinet below the sink, hoping the warm air would gradually defrost the drainpipe overnight. And this morning, believe it or not, the sink was empty, which made me wish you were here again, extolling, "My hero! My hero!" But I wonder what you'd have said just an hour or so later, when I tried to get rid of the airlock in the living room radiator and unscrewed the metal stopper so far that boiling hot water came spraying out, arcing across the width of the room, drenching books, newspapers, tape cassettes, the wooden floor, the oriental rug, the love seat, the speaker cabinets — everything in that corner of the room but the big black vase holding your ashes. The water was so hot that I couldn't screw the stopper back in without running to the kitchen for a pair of gloves, while Puck was scuttering around the living room floor, trying to lick up the water. Half an hour later, the stopper back in, the water mopped up, the newspapers trashed, the books and tapes and cabinets dried, I settled down for a late breakfast, a sigh of relief, and a memory of how you and I coped with the broken pipe that flooded the kitchen floor two years ago on New Year's Eve, in the middle of a long-distance call from cousin David. Some things never end.

SATURDAY, JANUARY 25

Dear Kate,

I'm having a hard time today, a very hard time, and I don't know why. Maybe because Trudy's gone, and I miss her companionship. Maybe because it's Saturday, and Saturdays keep reminding me of the day you died. Maybe because I had dinner last night at Cecile and Ruedi's — another collegial gathering — and found myself so enchanted by their lovely home and their loving ease with each other that every sip of his Côtes du Rhône and every bite of her beef bourguignon set my teeth on edge with envy. And it wasn't any better when I beheld David beaming across the table at Rebecca as she held forth about her ministerial duties, and Jack beaming at Mary Lynn when she talked about helping a young woman learn how to read. Only Carol, still grieving for her loss of Pierre, made me feel as if I were not alone. Such a bitter kind of solace that I'm ashamed to admit it. But then again, maybe I'm having a bad day because I noticed your sewing machine still in the corner of the dining room, where you put it the day before you died — a glance this morning that brought back the image of you hunched over the machine, making one beautiful thing after another, a silk dress for yourself, a wool shirt for me, a Christmas hanging for Hannah. But then again, maybe it's none of the above — maybe it's that no matter how often I write, you seem more distant today than you did several weeks ago, so for all I know you might be galaxies away a month or two from now. When I talked to my brother Marshall this afternoon, he told me that eventually I'll "get you back," that I'll "get some of you back" and then you'll "be with me forever." And a few days ago when I was taking Puck for his sunset walk and Linda was lighting candles for you in the park, she told me, "It'll transform. It will. Just you wait and see. And when it does, then she'll be with you, she'll be part of you, and she'll always be with you." I couldn't help wondering just then how long that will be. And she replied, "Oh, that'll take awhile yet, I don't know how long, but it'll be awhile." So for the time being, I'm having a bad day, and there's nothing I can do to make it stop, except to stop thinking about it (and you).

SUNDAY, JANUARY 26

Dear Kate,

How can I stop thinking of you when friends call and want to talk, especially longtime friends like Jo Ann? She called this morning and reminisced about our week last fall in Barrington with her and Bob, and then our weekend together in Boston and the tour you took us on through Mount Auburn cemetery. So memorable that I could see you again in my mind's eye, in your blue denim jumper and your white blouse and your white sunhat, see you pulling out a map from the information booth at the entryway, then mulling over a route through the maze of walkways, then heading down one of the central paths, all of us in tow, identifying trees and shrubs and flowers along the way. A vivid memory, so pleasant to recall, that it led me to think perhaps I've not been paying enough attention to our recent times together, except for the day you died, and perhaps that's why you seem to be slipping away, becoming more distant with every passing day. So I've pulled out a batch of shots from the past few years, and now I can see you holding forth at Holly's wedding reception last August, your mouth partly open, your eyes alert, gesturing with one hand, a wine goblet in the other, all decked out in your handmade dress from the blue and white Japanese cloth you bought in Hawaii. And here's another from a few months earlier, where I can see you sitting in your favorite place at the end of the couch, magazine in hand, looking quizzically at Jag, who's perched by your side on the arm of the couch. And here's another from last spring, of you and cousin David standing in front of the hollyhocks at the end of the driveway, both of you so bright-eyed and rosy-cheeked that despite his baldness and your head of hair, I can finally see the family resemblance. So close you could almost be brother and sister. But maybe I shouldn't be bringing you to mind like this, keeping my grief more fresh than I can bear. Or so I gather from Connie, who called after dinner this evening, checking up on me as she does every Sunday, like a savvy counselor rather than a longtime friend. But then again, I haven't shed a tear all day, so maybe I'm do-ing exactly what I should be doing, which makes me wonder if there are rules and regulations for the management of grief, and I'm just now discovering them by accident.

TUESDAY, JANUARY 28

Dear Kate,

Yesterday I tried to find some of the tea that we bought in China — I wanted to serve it with an Asian dinner that I planned for Lara, a for-mer graduate student, who's back in town the next several months and called to see how I'm doing. But no matter where I looked — in the kitchen cupboards, the corner cabinet, the basement fruit room, the suitcase we brought back from China, imploring your help at every turn — I couldn't find any of the tea. And I still can't find it. Today, at last, I've come to terms with the loss, figuring that you either gave it away, threw it away, or put it away somewhere that's beyond my ken. But yesterday, its inexplicable disappearance seemed like such a cruel little echo of your death that it sent me into a nosedive until it was time to make dinner, set the table, and put on a good face for Lara. By the time she left, I was so exhausted that I didn't have the energy to write you a letter. Today, on the other hand, I buried my sorrow in the monthly bills and revisions for my share of the freshman textbook. "Keep busy" is what the lady at the gas station told me this noon, when I asked how she had dealt with the deaths of her husband and both of her children. I didn't realize that she knew you or me by name, until she told me how saddened she was by the news of your death. So I kept busy today, mindful of others who've lost far more than I.

FRIDAY, JANUARY 31

Dear Kate,

Three days without crying — I can hardly believe it. Oh yes, I've been thinking of you every day, and every day I've had a few momen-tary chills and shudders. But nothing like what happened last Saturday and Monday. In fact, the past few days have been such a far cry (no pun intended) from the past nine or ten weeks that I'm wondering what it means, or what's happened to produce this sudden calmness.

At first, I thought it might mean that I was beginning to get over your death, but so soon that it made me wonder about the depth of my caring. "Don't worry," said my brother, who called early this afternoon. "You'll probably find yourself crying again and again. What you're going through now is just part of the process." He didn't say exactly what he meant by that, but it sure is nice to have a temporary break, a time to catch my breath before it starts all over again. Maybe it's also a response to the extremity of what happened on Monday — "After great pain a formal feeling comes — The nerves sit ceremonious like tombs . . ." But that's not exactly how I'm feeling, so much as that I'm in something like a state of suspended animation, emotionally on hold, you might say. I also think it might be the result of having been so busy the past few days, finishing work on the textbook, that my mind has been somewhere else. This afternoon I mailed in the manuscript, so I wonder if the end of that task might leave me vulnerable again. But then again, having devised all those questions for the anthologized readings, I now have to supply the answers for the instructors' manual. So I have another two weeks of work and potential distractions. Whoever thought that hackwork could be so restorative?

I'm also feeling better today because this morning, right before breakfast, I found the missing Chinese tea that led to my breakdown on Monday — found it in your big copper pot where I should have realized it would be in the first place. But when I first looked up at the pot, sitting on the shelf above the kitchen counter, almost as shiny as when you polished it the day before you died, something made me dismiss it as an unlikely storage place for the tea. Maybe because I'd never seen you put the tea in there to begin with. But this morning, when I noticed the little clay teapots that we bought at the night market in Hangzhou, sitting next to the pot, it suddenly occurred to me that the tea might be nearby. So I lifted down the pot, took off the lid, and lo! there they were — all the cartons and canisters of tea, still as aromatic, it seemed, as when we bought the stuff some three years ago. For a moment, just then, it felt as if I had found a treasure chest, a sacred cache, the makings of a magical potion, an elixir of life, you name it. For a moment just then, I could also feel something like a smile overtaking my face — a rare feeling. So, to celebrate my good fortune, I made myself a pot of jasmine tea, and I've been feeling restored ever since. Now if only you were hidden away in plain sight.

SATURDAY, FEBRUARY I

Dear Kate,

Holly and Lain are coming for dinner, so I spent the day in a flurry of domesticity, keeping my grief at bay with the vacuum, a feather duster, and all the chop-chop for a Chinese New Year's dinner. Now that everything's ready to cook, I'm sitting here in the kitchen, tapping out this letter, remembering how radiant you looked when we dined at Adagio the night before you died. A strange thing, you might say, to be remembering right now. Actually, I've been thinking about it since Thursday, when I dined at Adagio with Caroline and Len. Though I've been there several times with them the past two months, something about Thursday night made me remember our dinner with Gene. I think it was the seating arrangement — Len and I sitting next to each other in a booth, directly across from Caroline, much as Gene and I were sitting next to each other, directly across from you. Isn't it strange how something as trivial as that can trigger a memory? Cognitive psychologists could probably give me chapter and verse to explain how analogous patterns trigger associative recall, but whatever the cause, I've been remembering how you glowed that evening right from the start, from the minute you came downstairs in your black velvet outfit and white blouse. At first, I thought it was the outfit, but then I saw a glow on your cheeks, a brightness in your eyes that never faded, even when you were critiquing the mashed potatoes and gorgonzola cheese that came with your beef tenderloin, critiquing them with your usual wit and verve. Something about the color in your cheeks and the look in your eyes was like nothing I'd ever seen in you before, as if you were on cloud nine. I didn't want to say anything in front of Gene, lest I make you self-conscious. So I kept my peace, and the next day swept everything into the background. Now I can't help wondering what mysterious thing was glowing in you that evening. The light before the dark? Some intuition or premonition on your part? Or just an optical illusion or trick of my imagination?

A few nights ago when I looked out the kitchen window, I saw that Linda had made her most flamboyant display since you died — seven candles arranged in the shape of a gigantic V, encompassing almost a third of the park. And no sooner did I see that V-shaped arrangement than I thought she was sending me a message of sorts, a V-for-victory sign to buoy me up. But when I walked over to the park with Puck, I discovered that the candles were arranged in a semicircle, that the gigantic V was just an optical illusion. Anymore, I'm not sure about any-thing I'm seeing or remembering. But it sure was a pleasure to see that V again when I got back home. And to think of your radiance again.

Dear Kate,

Sometimes I wonder how you'd be doing if I had died, and the first thing that comes to mind is how you cried yourself to sleep every night after my heart attack when I was in the hospital recovering from the triple bypass. "But I wouldn't have written about it like this," I can hear you saying, "not day in and day out." No, that surely wouldn't have been your way. Far from it, I imagine you'd have grieved aplenty but kept it to yourself (and your poems), much as you didn't tell me about your crying until months after my heart attack, and then only in passing as part of another memory. Come to think of it, you were much too busy then to write, what with shuttling back and forth to the hospital, then nursing me back to health with daily walks, a heart-healthy diet, and your irrepressible zest for life. And then to top it all off, building me a three-bin composter with the help of your sister Martha — an incomparable gift for my return to the garden. A new life after a near-death experience, the thought of which leaves me all the more anguished that I could do nothing to save your life, except in letters like this bearing witness to it.

Sometimes I wonder how you'd be doing if I had died, and all I can say for sure is that you'd be doing it with far more dignity (and privacy) than I.

THURSDAY, FEBRUARY 6

Dear Kate,

I got a call last night from Valerie, who now resides in an assisted living center in Santa Cruz, where the average age of her cohorts is somewhere in the late eighties. It's hard to believe that Valerie is now in an assisted-living center. But the thing that sticks in my mind is her recollection of how you used to call me by my last name. "I just loved it, just loved how she always called you Klaus, right to your face. The first time I heard her do it, it took me utterly by surprise. And then I couldn't wait to hear her do it again. And she always dragged it out a bit — Klaaauuus — so it sounded like she was exasperated or putting you in your place." For a moment just then, it was almost as if I could hear your voice again, her imitation was so good. She's not the only one who's remembered, especially among the old-timers, but her imitation got me thinking again about why you did it. At first, I was taken by surprise, but didn't want to ask lest I spoil the sport of it and the magic. And then it gradually became so habitual that I didn't give it a second thought. But I remember myself thinking at the start that you might be avoiding my first name, because it would have sounded too familiar, too personal, especially since I was a faculty member and you a graduate student. "I'm keeping a proper distance," you seemed to be saying, as if to call me Carl would have been presumptuous or put you in peril of being too intimate. But gradually things began to change, and so did the meaning of my last name, like the first time I picked you up and carried you through the front door of your parents' home, and then suddenly your exclamation of "Klaaauuus" seemed to say, "What in the world do you think you're doing?!" And later still it turned into a form of reproof, and by degrees it seemed capable of signifying almost anything from exasperation to affection to elation, and everything in between. But probably I'm telling you things you already know too well. It's just that the recollection of them is so delicious I want to remember even more. Like how it never really worked when I called you by your last name, probably because "Franks" can't be dragged out at all without sounding whiny, as you probably knew the first time you heard me try it.

Still, you can hardly imagine how much I wanted to invoke your name, whine it out in my loudest voice — "Fraaaanks!" — when I was listening to the United Airlines specialist as she explained the letters I have to write and the documentation I have to provide in order to get your accumulated miles transferred to my account and get a refund for your unused ticket to Hawaii.

FRIDAY, FEBRUARY 7

Dear Kate,

The bitterly cold weather, our quarreling pets, the ringing telephone, our falling real-estate stock — it was a day of downers. But nothing got to me quite like the call from my nephew David. He'd just returned home from seeing my brother receive an award in New York

City, and he wanted to give me an update on how well he looks now that it's more than six months since his stroke. Good news for sure, and I was glad to hear it. The only problem was that I couldn't get him to see how risky it was for his father to fly from California to New York, how the blood pools on long-distance flights in ways that can lead to blood clots that can lead to strokes. For he kept on telling me how much better he looked than last summer, as if his physical appearance were proof against a stroke. That's what really got to me so much that I suddenly couldn't resist telling him (or nearly yelling at him) how absolutely beautiful you looked the night before you died and just minutes before your stroke and even when you were dying in the hospital. And then I vowed to keep my mouth shut and not do that to myself any more.

But just to assure you that the day was not a complete loss, I went to the city park department this afternoon and reserved the Seiberling Grove for your memorial service. So, as things now stand, the service will take place exactly where you wished, on Sunday, May 25, the day before Memorial Day. The other good news is that the photocopying place made me a special notecard, showing you in the middle of your perennial bed, a big smile on your face, both of your arms outstretched, a pitchfork in one hand, your other in a V-for-victory sign. I plan to use the cards to thank the many people who contributed to your memorial fund, especially since the picture makes it look like you're thanking them too.

MONDAY, FEBRUARY 10

Dear Kate,

A woman called this afternoon asking in a very pleasant voice, "May I please speak to Kate?" Such a disarming request that I was momentarily nonplussed and then said, "She's not alive." How's that for a strange expression? A circumlocution, as if I didn't want to say you're dead, though God knows I've been saying that or words to that effect in almost every one of these letters. I've also been reporting your death to other people whenever I call or write to various businesses or governmental agencies. So why didn't I just say it directly? "She's dead." Perhaps, because I've never said it that bluntly, not even when I called Amy after you died and told her, "She's gone." And maybe because I don't want to concede your death, your nonexistence, in such a definitive way as that. Otherwise, I might also have to admit the absurdity of this project, of writing letters to someone who's dead. And I might have to concede a lot of other things as well, say, like you don't really figure in my life anymore, though you're still on my mind more often than when you were alive.

Just to show you how conflicted I am when it comes to talking about your death, here's another story from this morning, featuring Steve from the Appliance Barn. Today, more than four months after he first worked on the cooktop and you told him about the malfunctioning burner, he finally had all the parts in hand to fix it. And as usual he arrived with that winning smile on his face, but a smile that seemed to contain a question or a hint of uneasiness. I too had a welcoming smile on my face, but a smile that also must have contained a hint of uneasiness, for I didn't know whether I should say anything about your absence. And from then on it was a strange hour or so, each of us smiling wordlessly at the other, as he did his repairs and I worked on the instructors' manual for the textbook. Both of us were still smiling when he left, especially after he fixed the burner so well that it works like new. But now I'm wondering if he knew, yet didn't want to say anything until I brought it up myself. As in, don't offend the customers by mentioning something that they don't want to talk about. And even if he did (or didn't) know, why didn't I say something to explain what surely must have been on his mind, given all the times he's been here when you were alive. And why for that matter haven't I written your friend James, or my friend Skippy, to tell them about it? Emotional fatigue? Avoidance? Or a way of keeping you alive, at least so far as they are concerned? Dead or alive, it sure is a strange way to be.

FRIDAY, FEBRUARY 14
Dear Valentine,

What I remember about this holiday is that you cherished it as if it were your own special day, or your birthday, just twelve days later. So in days of yore, when February was upon us, my days were consumed by deeds of love — by the need to make you a colorful valentine, write you a witty poem to be incorporated in the valentine, and procure a captivating present, while also imagining new and ingenious ways to celebrate your upcoming birthday. So many duties, so little time, that the month of February always made me feel as if I were being tested again and again, like a knight errant, to see if my love, my ardor, would rise to the occasion. Whereas you, blithely it seemed, managed to craft a valentine, write a poem, and bake me a cherry pie, as if doing so were a mere bagatelle. The cherries were always ready in the freezer from last year's crop; your paper doilies were always on hand in the corner cupboard; and your muse was always on duty. So while I labored to bring forth a tortured little ditty, you called forth hearts and arrows, cupids and kisses, as if the language of love were yours and yours alone. Given such a deflating contest of wits, you'd think the end of it would bring a gigantic sigh of relief. But no, nothing of the kind has issued from yours truly. Au contraire, he moped around the house this morning, bereft at the thought that this day would come and go without his valentine pie. But the mail did, after all, bring him a valentine from Martha, a cheery picture of ripe red tomatoes that she had cut in the shape of a heart, outlined in black like the ruffled edge of a doily and overlaid with a bright green arrow also outlined in black. And so he thought his Valentine's Day was complete, until a surprise package arrived on the front porch from White Flower Farm. Momentarily, he thought it might be something from his departed valentine, a midwinter surprise, ordered before she died. But no, it was a consolatory gift, featuring a dozen pips of your beloved lilies of the valley, together with a shapely clay pot and potting soil for planting and bringing them on in the house. After potting them up and centering the pot on top of the dining room plant-stand, he thought his Valentine's Day complete. But no, another surprise arrived shortly before dinner, when Trudy called, "just checking in," completely oblivious of this special day, until he reminded her of it, and then she was all apologies. "Oh, I should have known, I should have known, I remember her sending me a special handmade valentine, and how much it pleased me." And that, dear Valentine, is exactly what yours truly was feeling all day long, all day long.

SUNDAY, FEBRUARY 16

Dear Kate,

Hannah called this morning, as she often does on Sunday, and we talked quite awhile. She said I sounded depressed — probably because I was crying off and on during the conversation. She in turn was trying to get me out of my funk by offering some thoughtful observations and suggestions. Not surprising, given her work with grieving parents and children. From what she said, I'm evidently trying to hold on to you too tightly, as if letting go might send me plummeting into an abyss. She probably got that impression from some of these letters that I e-mailed her last week. And I can't disagree with her diagnosis, seeing as how I keep writing you every day and looking at shots of you almost every day. I just found the ones from our trip to China, and was blown away by the image of us standing side-by-side at the stern of our riverboat, all got up in our green raingear and confident smiles, the Yangtze gorges looming up in the mist behind us. But I know that Hannah's thinking about something other than snapshots and letters — an obsessive state of mind, which I'd love to be free of, given how wonderful it is when someone or something takes me far afield. And that's what she said will happen when I go to Florida next week, when I leave this memory-filled house, and go to a place I've never seen before. So in a strange sort of way, I'm looking forward to it even as I'm a little uneasy about it. Maybe I wouldn't be holding on so fiercely if I hadn't been orphaned so young, hadn't come to feel that you gave me a home and a love like I'd never had before — and will never have again. I don't think Hannah realized that connection until we were talking today, and then she understood why I was holding on so tight, but still felt that letting go would ultimately make me more secure. A paradox that appeals to my literary sensibility, especially when I put it in the form of an epigram — "Letting go is the surest way of holding on."

WEDNESDAY, FEBRUARY 19

Dear Kate,

I just got home from a meeting of the preservation board, and the first thing I noticed was an extraordinary display of lights in the park, far more than when I left shortly after dinner. At first, there were just four candles, but now there are eight more, arranged like a huge diamond extending from one end of the park to the other. It looks like Linda's gone all out tonight, inspired perhaps by an anonymous gift of candles, which she told me about yesterday — people have evidently been leaving them under the park sign. I don't know what she's up to, except that the display changes every night, and recently it's been quite attractive up close, because she builds little snow forts to protect the candles, so their flickering light radiates around the snow. And you were wondering whether anyone would remember you?

THURSDAY, FEBRUARY 20

Dear Kate,

Here's an update on last night's candle display, which didn't look at all like a diamond when I saw it up close — instead, just two rows of candles five to ten feet apart. So different that at first it seemed as if I might be having a problem with depth perception. But when I walked toward the street and then looked back to the park, I noticed that the candles seemed different from that angle too. So it seems there's no single way of seeing the candles, even up close, which makes me wonder how they'd appear if I were looking directly down at them from twenty or thirty feet in midair. Yes, yes, I can hear your sarcastic question, "So what else is new in Epistemology 101?" But it's strange how I keep forgetting those basic truths in matters close to home, like the candles in the park or you. And now that you're gone, now that it's impossible to see you at all, I wonder all the more about what I'm seeing or remembering, especially from such a distance as now divides us.

As if to heighten the problem, Marshall called today, seemingly in a mood to reminisce about you and how serious you always seemed to be. And I quickly replied, "But Kate wasn't always that serious — in fact she was often quite playful, whimsical, ready for a good time and ready to give it her all." But then he reminded me how stern you sometimes were when he was growing up, and then I reminded him of how little he'd seen you the last twenty-five years. And around we went, each of us clinging to his own perception of you, though he did recall your playful gifts of recent years. But no sooner had I gotten off the phone than I began to think of how little I myself might have known you, given how much of the time we were apart — and not just when I was at work, but also when we were at home, doing our separate things. What were you up to, what were you thinking, I wonder, when we weren't face-to-face across the dinner table or in bed or traveling together? Now come to think of it, I remember how inscrutable you sometimes seemed to be — so much so that I'd occasionally ask what was on your mind, and with a twinkle in your eye you'd say, "If I want you to know, I'll tell you." Which put me in mind of the spare and tantalizing comments you wrote for the thirtieth-anniversary yearbook of your college class. Just a brief caption identifying the time and place of each snapshot, followed by a single remark and a cheery farewell: "Any more you want to know (to use the Midwestern idiom) may not be your business. Cheers!" Now it all comes back, and I remember when you were planning your page that you didn't want to make a list of your accomplishments or tell the story of your life since college or anything else in that self-regarding vein. But I'd forgotten how elusive you chose to be. And now you're more so than ever before.

SATURDAY, FEBRUARY 22

Dear Kate,

The past few weeks I've had some trouble keeping a hold on myself — and I don't mean emotionally. That goes without saying. I'm talking quite literally about holding on to my self, to a clear-cut sense of who I am, now that you're gone. A strange sense of disorientation that I haven't felt since I retired. But that — the loss of my professional identity — was nothing compared to this. For now it seems as if I've lost the very ground of my being, having thought of myself for so many, many years as inseparable from you. And not just in the conventional sense of "to have and to hold 'til death do us part," but in the existential sense of to be who I am and have known myself to be ever since I've known you. Yes, I can hear your cautionary words of long ago — "We're becoming too interdependent, too symbiotic. After all, we're not joined at the hip." But I can also remember my rejoinder, as in, "What's wrong with symbiosis, if it's mutually beneficial?" Now, of course, I can see what might be wrong, though I don't think it was death that worried you back then, so much as a concern with your own sense of identity. As if you worried that it might not be possible to retain a sense of your self in a marriage that was so mutually involving as ours. But you did, forever facing me down with the fierceness of your hold on reality and your no-nonsense response to the absurdity of things that crossed your path. Whereas I relied so much on you (and your reality checks) that I never saw myself apart from you — until now. So who am I anyway? Not any longer your husband, though I'm still wearing the wedding band, so tight that I couldn't get it off if I wanted to. A widower for sure, in the usual parlance. But mostly someone still so shaped by you and all you stood for that I sometimes feel like a thing of your making, a character in one of your plays, a creation that you never stopped writing until your final exit. No wonder I keep studying your life — how else can I know who I am?

SUNDAY, FEBRUARY 23

Dear Kate,

Your cousin Mary and Larry were in town yesterday for their annual basketball weekend — the first time I'll have seen them since the four of us went to the game last year. So I spent the day cleaning house and putting together a dinner for them last night. You, of course, were the center of attention, though at first you were upstaged by Puck, who was so fondled and flattered by Mary that he might well have abandoned me and gone home with her and Larry. I'd forgotten her mania for dogs. But I also didn't realize that you were a favorite of Mary and her brother Pete — he loved your spunk, and she always wanted a sister, a sister just like you. So she was delighted by the things that I gave her — your onyx necklace, your black velvet purse, and one of your silk scarves. But the real hit of the evening — aside from Puck and the beef tenderloins — were your modeling pictures. I didn't realize that Larry and Mary were living in Omaha when you were modeling in New York and San Francisco, so they never saw you during that time. Nor had they ever seen any of your modeling shots and clipsheets, which completely surprised them, especially the one of you all gussied up in a Chanel-type suit and dashing hat, posing at a construction site and a chemical refinery plant — "Just look at that face! She had the classic features! And look at how she could strike all those poses, just like that! Why didn't she continue modeling?" It took a little explaining, but when I told them about all the makeup and the manipulation and the anorexic thinness, I think they had second thoughts, but still "the glamour of having a cousin who looked like that" was irresistibly appealing, as I know myself from having been married to a woman who looked like that.

MONDAY, FEBRUARY 24

Dear Kate,

From sunrise to sunset, I worked myself into a frenzy with the seed orders, for everything has to be on hand when I get back from Florida, otherwise I won't have seedlings ready for transplant in April. Can you hear the urgency of a compulsive in those stress-ridden sentences? I thought it would be a simple matter — just check my cache of seed packets, see what needs to be replenished, go to the catalogs, make out the orders, and phone them in. But no sooner did I start going through my seeds than I started to choke up. The first time in two days. And it wasn't just the converted tackle box you gave me with its homey filing system, but also the memories of your favorite vegetables. Like the Green Arrow peas, and the Ichiban eggplants, and the Golden Sunray tomatoes. Midway through the vegetables, I realized that I'd also have to order the herb and flower seeds which you always did on your own. And start the seedlings for those too. That's when I really caved in — and not because of the added work but the memory of your hands, your elegant fingers, fussing delicately over your seeds and seed trays. If it hadn't been for a call just then, I might still be in tears. It was Trudy, wanting me to know how delighted and moved she was by the thank-you card with the picture of you in your perennial bed. Sometimes I don't know what I'd do without her phone calls and visits.

WEDNESDAY, FEBRUARY 26

Dear Kate,

What a strange way to celebrate your birthday — not with flowers and gifts but with wills and property lists. Signing this and photocopying that, documenting this and detailing that, so that all our assets can easily be found and distributed in the event of my death. A far cry from last year's festivities, when you posed for snapshots, sporting your dark sunglasses and the black lei from Martha, your hands arched over the black wreath she sent, as if in mourning for yourself. A theatrical performance par excellence. Who could have imagined that such a playful scene would turn out to be a haunting premonition?

A strange day made stranger still by the sudden blackout of my laptop computer. So much for my plans to keep writing you while in Florida. Yes, I can hear your predictable question — "What's wrong with paper and pencil?" The same question that the aging repairman asked me when I took it to him this morning. And it didn't get any better, given all the errands to be done — like money from the bank, aloha shirts from the drycleaner's, wine for Gene from the liquor store, jewelry for Martha from your safe deposit box, and laptop again from the repair center. Now, in fact, I'm so exhausted from the day that I can hardly wait to be airborne, then seaside, far, far away from this vale of tears.

THURSDAY, FEBRUARY 27

Dear Kate,

It sure was a pleasure to see Martha at the airport this afternoon, a sudden smile on her face when she saw me coming down the escalator, a shy but bright-eyed grin so much like yours it took me by surprise and reminded me again of ties that run deeper than anyone could fathom. Then a momentary glance at each other, and both of us agreed that we look much better than either of us might have imagined. The way she put it was, "I'm glad to see that you're taking good care of yourself." And my response was, "Can you imagine what she'd do if I let myself go?" Yes, in some part of my head I still live in fear of your reproof, as if the force of your will had outlived you. And then we headed across the bay to Largo, where we've been hanging out all afternoon, over turkey sandwiches, beer, and memories of you. Memories sparked by those pictures of you, posing with all the wacky gifts she sent last year. I thought she should see them, painful as it was. And some other memories occasioned by the jewelry of yours that I gave her today, especially the black and white Mondrianish brooch that you bought at the art fair right before you died. I've had it on display in the dining room, like a sacred token of your last morning, and a reminder of how delighted you were when you showed it to me just minutes before the onset of your stroke. But it's time now for Martha to have the pin and wear it, seeing as how it's so akin to her angular artwork. She's wearing it on her sweatshirt right now, ready to leave for dinner at a nearby restaurant, looking like she was meant to have it all along.

FRIDAY, FEBRUARY, 28

Dear Kate,

Largo is just like you said — miles and miles of strip malls. And palm trees galore. A strange combination, though probably I shouldn't be surprised, given a similar disconnect in Honolulu. Speaking of disconnects, last night Martha and Lynn took me to one of their favorite seafood places, with the unpromising name of Guppy's, but the fish was far grander than the name. And this morning she took me to her neighborhood park, where we saw a slew of red-eared turtles, basking in the sun, also an elegant egret, hunting, she said, for geckoes. And just a bit later, I saw a gecko myself. All I lacked was a gator up close and personal, and my day would have been complete, especially after a tour of her tropical poolside garden. She also surprised me with a bunch of snapshots I'd never seen before — pictures of you and me from before we were married, from our wedding day, as well as from the trip she took with us to Puget Sound. So many years ago, all of us so young and hopeful, it seemed like another life. It also seemed like another life when she showed me a few of the paper lanterns that you got in Shanghai just a few years ago, the day before we flew to Honolulu — I can still see you buying them from a street merchant on our way back to the Peace Hotel. No wonder we both had a good cry after lunch, which moved her to say something I've not heard from anyone else — "It's so hard for me, I can't imagine what it must be like for you to get up every morning and face the emptiness every day." And that moved her to cry even more at the thought of what her life would be like without Lynn. So much for the joys of travel. But then again, so much for the folly of thinking I could forget my dead wife by visiting her kid sister.

SATURDAY, MARCH 1

Dear Kate,

Last night in bed, I was thinking about my upcoming visit to Gene and the coincidence that brought him to visit us the weekend you died — how he wouldn't have come had it not been for John's brain tumor. And that made me think of another coincidence, of how I'd never have met you had John not hired me to teach at Iowa and you not come to study at the Writers' Workshop. And soon enough I was thinking of the destiny that shapes our ends, rough-hew them though we will. So, it's probably not surprising that I dreamt of you this morning and the dream began at John's back door. It was a Sunday morning, and there I was with a bundle of clothes strapped on my back, like a drifter looking for a handout. No sooner did I knock on the door than John invited me downstairs, where I found you sitting at a card table, waiting, it seemed, for a meal to be served (like an echo of you sitting primly at the table, when you were waiting for me to serve the dinner that I cooked for our first date). I excused myself briefly to wash up, but you were gone when I returned, and four men were sitting down at a table nearby, as if to start playing cards. (An allusion, perhaps, to the high stakes poker that I played during the years of our courtship.) Then the scene shifted, and we were together once again, chatting during the intermission of the Gershwin concert that we heard just a few weeks before you died. Then I turned my head for a moment, looking for a men's room, and the minute I turned back you were gone. But this time I couldn't find you, no matter where I looked — a search that left me more frantic than I've been in any other dream since you died. And even more desperate when I awoke. By this time, you'd think the disappearing-Kate dream was so familiar that I'd take it for granted. But this dream was far more inclusive, like an epitome of my entire life with you — from rags to riches to loss.

I told Martha about it, and she proposed a day of distractions, beginning with a Home Depot, where they're already selling tomato seedlings and bedding plants, two months ahead of us in Iowa. A tropical lure for sure. A tropical clothing store was also on the agenda, given the need of a sunhat for yours truly, who left his back in Iowa. Best of all was a barefoot walk along the gulf, sand under my feet the first time since you and I were in Hanalei last March. Martha talked about the danger of stingrays just offshore, but all I could think of were the perils of memory right along the beach, every shell a reminder of the specimens you gathered last spring. But the shudders I felt along the bay were nothing compared to a sudden onset of tears when Martha, Lynn, and I were leaving the Tampa Arena after a tennis match featuring Martina Navratilova and Tracy Austin. Nothing to do with you, nothing at all, except for the ominous-looking approach to a downward-moving escalator, inexorably carrying us to an invisible exit, emblem of the ultimate unknown. And that, of course, is when I broke down. A few more months of this, and maybe I'll be case-hardened to things like that.

SUNDAY, MARCH 2

Dear Kate,

I've been thinking about last night's tennis match, thanks to an article in this morning's newspaper, explaining why Austin was no match for Navratilova. How could she have been, given that Navratilova maintains a full competitive schedule, whereas before last night

Austin hadn't played a singles match in ten years, given her marriage and three children. Such different careers that I couldn't help thinking about the choices you made during our lives together. "All that matters to me," I remember your saying at first, "is our marriage, my writing, your children, and my family." You rattled them off so quickly they seemed like a manageable set of commitments, until the ambushes of life slowly but surely revealed the outlandishness of so many burdens. No wonder your playwriting fell by the wayside at first, but gradually flourished once my children were on their own, your mother had bounced back, and our social obligations diminished. Four full-length plays in five years and staged readings in Iowa City, Madison, and San Francisco, not to mention your published translations. Everything going your way, it seemed, until your comedy was rejected once too often, and you shoved the manuscript back in the envelope with the flat-out announcement — "'That's it, that's enough. I'll never write another play." I'll never forget how you answered me that night, when I urged you to reconsider: "Don't you realize that it's crazy to keep writing these plays if nobody wants to produce them? Would you keep writing essays if nobody wanted to publish them?" And so it was that your choices changed — from playwriting and translating to a host of other things so splendidly done that Martha was not exaggerating the other day when she called you a Renaissance woman. How strange, then, that you often spoke of having wasted your life in the latter days of your life. As if a full-length play, fully staged, were all that really mattered. As if that one talent lodged within you were truly death to hide.

MONDAY, MARCH 3

Dear Kate,

Largo yesterday, Key West today, and it suddenly feels like the tropics. Heat and humidity like I hadn't felt since last July. And it's only the beginning of March. No wonder Gene told me just to bring a pair of shorts and an aloha shirt. Imagine Hawaii without the trade winds and you'll know what it feels like. Imagine sixty thousand people on a little island, four miles long, one or two miles wide, and you'll get a sense of the crowding. Then add a stream of motorcycles and motor scooters, and you'll get a sense of what it sounds like. This is a noisy little place, the narrow streets of the commercial areas lined with tourist shops like so much flypaper, and the people swarming in and out of the stores like so many flies. But the residential areas are splendid — filled with nineteenth-century houses in every imaginable style, from Creole cottage to stately mansion, from one peaked roof to gables galore. An architectural delight, decked out with palm trees and flowering bougainvillea.

Best of all was the Audubon House, where I almost shed a few hundred bucks on a hand-colored lithograph of an Audubon goldfinch — the Iowa state bird for your trophy room — but in the middle of thumbing through a rack of pictures, I suddenly heard your cautionary voice, "But where are you going to hang it, when we don't even have room for the Rouault or any of the others that are sitting up in the attic?" And then I remembered how you chafed whenever I wanted to hang a few more things in the living room — "I don't want to live in a museum." So, instead of getting an Audubon, Gene and I went to pick up some meat for dinner. We found something you'd have loved — a pork tenderloin stuffed with provolone, prosciutto, and dried tomatoes that went very nicely with the red wine I brought from Iowa. Then back home for a dip in the pool — Gene swimming laps, Bobby getting her knees back in shape, and I floundering around like a flatlander. And then an evening of so much wine and so many good memories that I never felt too sorry for myself, not even when I woke up four hours later with a fierce hangover.

TUESDAY, MARCH 4

Dear Kate,

My hangover is over, and now that it's bedtime the heat and humidity have also abated. Somewhat. But the air was oppressive again this afternoon when Gene and I went to scope out the Key West Garden Club. A dazzling array of tropical flora overlooking the sea — orchids, cycads, bromeliads, gingers, banyans, palms — and all I could think of was the heat, the insufferable heat. As bad as it was that time we got off the plane in New Orleans, and you never stopped sweating the whole week we were there.

This evening, though, the ramshackle place where we dined was so comfortably air-conditioned I could have stayed there all night, sipping my sauvignon blanc. Such an extensive list of entrees, I hardly knew what to choose, until Gene noticed a seafood stew, and I remembered your love of bouillabaisse and cioppino, remembered the ones you ordered wherever we went — Cincinnati, Monterey, Sausalito, San Francisco, Mobile. But this one was different from any you ever had or made — a composed dish rather than a soup, including eight dark-shelled mussels (I counted them), next to four gray-shelled clams, offset by two large shrimp and several pieces of red snapper, tinctured reddish orange by the roasted tomato sauce, filled with bits of andouille that bordered the other side of the white bowl. So striking and tasty that we wound up talking about the great fish stews of our past, which put me in mind of the one you made last fall, complete with croûtes and a pungent rouille. I promised to send Bobby your recipe. Come to think of it, there's a little bit left in the freezer, awaiting my return.

WEDNESDAY, MARCH 5

Dear Kate,

The National Park Service flyer assured us that "your trip to the Dry Tortugas will be an adventure." What it didn't say was that "it will also be a torture," thanks to the pitch and roll of the waves that made me feel like barfing all the way there and back — seventy miles each way. So much for the purported stability of a catamaran. And when I wasn't nauseated, I was imagining how much worse it would have been for you. But once Gene and I arrived, it was a rare pleasure from start to finish. A tiny island, no more than twenty-five hundred feet around, containing one of the largest forts in the world, built in the mid nineteenth century with sixteen million bricks shipped in from Florida, and God knows how much granite from New England. Crenellated, decked out with several hundred cannon sites, and surrounded by a moat. Such a formidable-looking place that its romanesque façade was enough to intimidate pirates. Standing on that little speck of land, looking at that three-story extravaganza, I suddenly found myself remembering the time you took the measure of our home for your long-distance architectural drafting course. I can still see you bent over your drafting board in the attic, drawing every brick in the façade, one by one, rather than just producing a sample inset, as your architectural advisor suggested. No shortcuts for you. Given such care, how could I ever forget you?

The only problem is that I wonder how other people feel about the way I keep bringing you up in conversation. This evening, for example, when I was telling Bobby and Gene about who's come and gone since they left Iowa City, I couldn't help noticing how often I referred to you and me. It's still "Kate and I" so often, especially when I'm with old friends like them, that I wonder if it sounds like I'm trying to keep you alive in language, as if the mere invocation of your name might bring you back again, as in a sense it does. So I wonder what others are thinking when I talk that way. And I wonder how long it'll keep happening before I can bring myself to stop. Something I don't want to do for fear of stifling the little of you that is left in my life.

FRIDAY, MARCH 7

Dear Kate,

The minute I came down for breakfast, Gene asked, "Do you ever get those retired-professor nightmares?" I knew what he meant — the anxiety dream of missing classes or losing student papers for an entire course. But I haven't had such a dream since you died. Now, as I told him, my nightmares are completely different, and the telling brought tears to my eyes — the first time since I arrived on Monday. But a tour of the Little White House with Bobby was a perfect distraction, thanks to some fascinating stories and pictures of Truman in Key West. You'd have enjoyed the 1940s decor, a delightful combination of tropical bamboo and colonial furniture. And I was captivated by a mahogany poker table, handmade for Truman by Navy carpenters, with slots for poker chips, ashtrays made of armor shells, and a parquet surface to conceal the poker stuff whenever Bess wanted to host a bridge game or luncheon. But the thing that really caught my eye was a picture of Harry sitting at an upright piano with a big grin on his face, and Lauren Bacall sitting almost expressionless on top of the piano, in a tropical suit, legs alluringly crossed to promote the movie version of Hemingway's *To Have and Have Not*. The minute I saw it, I remembered the tropical suit you made for Amy's high school graduation, and the picture of you in that suit, striding so confidently that when Amy saw it she dubbed you her "foxy stepmom." Yet now that I'm back in Largo, the thing that gets me most of all is neither your suit, nor Bacall's, nor Truman's grin, nor his handmade poker table, nor anything else I saw or did or thought or felt in Key West. Everything suddenly as transient and insubstantial as a dream, even Bobby and Gene, whom I might never see again for all I know.

This morning at breakfast, Gene was musing over the layers of distortion involved in dreaming, then in recalling a dream at the moment of awakening, then in putting one's memories of the dream into words — until he and I were laughing at the absurdity of it all. A dream is one thing and memory quite another. But who's to say where one begins and the other ends?

SATURDAY, MARCH 8
Dear Kate,

I'm now in Sarasota, and it's nearly bedtime or dreamtime, and I'm dizzy from the swirl of flying back to Tampa yesterday afternoon, then driving down here this morning with Martha, then lunching with Lynda and Ron at their favorite seafood place (a pastel wonderland of lavender shrimp and pink turtles swimming on pale turquoise walls, the waiters all in black), then touring another tropical garden center, then walking a beach where I was almost undone again by memories of you looking for shells in Kauai, in China, in Canada, on the shores of Lake Michigan, on the gulf at Destin — so many spots in time converged in a single moment that I was already dazed before we dined at poolside on a large glass table, lit by the moon and an extravagant chandelier, drinking beer, then wine, then God knows what, as we solved so many problems of youth and age and the state of the country that we rewarded ourselves with a quick trip to a local bistro for a batch of key lime pie. *Sic transit gloria mundi.*

SUNDAY, MARCH 9
Dear Kate,

When I got up this morning, Ron was in the sunroom, bent over a spiral notebook, working on a cartoon — a pleasant surprise to see that he's still drawing, given how Parkinson's has affected his motor control. I couldn't help wondering if I'd be doing so well with such a hobbling disease. I also wondered whether I'd be doing as well as Lynda, had you been similarly impaired. They've got a hard road in front of them, but they're both smiling. So it was a pleasure to sit by the poolside table, breaking the fast with mangoes and croissants, listening to Lynda's captivating stories — stories of friends whose venturesome lives had me thinking about Lynda herself, who surely could have been a successful writer but evidently chose instead to be not only a teacher but also a storyteller, a raconteur par excellence. *Chacun à son goût*— as I discovered again this afternoon when we went to see *Frida* at the local cineplex. At first I was struck by her youthful rebellion against everything in her family and everything in her culture — as if she were defining herself, creating herself, by opposition. As if her life itself were a radical work of art. Then I was struck by the ferocity of her will to survive in the wake of a bone-crushing accident and long-suffering recovery that's shown in such graphic (and surrealistic) detail that it seems to have been a profoundly transforming experience. But ultimately, I was fascinated most of all by the self-absorption of her art, so fixated from start to finish upon images of herself in a world of fantastic settings as to have made a mythology of her life. And who's to say which is more consequential — the solipsism of her vision or the revolutionary art of her husband, Diego Rivera. In the end, I suppose, it's all a matter of who's looking or listening or reading. So I keep writing, with dreams of catching your ear.

MONDAY, MARCH 10
Dear Kate,

Martha and I drove back to Largo after yesterday's movie, her eyes on the destination like a jockey intent upon the finish line. A no-nonsense driver like you, always at the speed limit or just a bit above. "They're holding dinner for us" is the way she put it, as we raced through a torrential rain. And today she's been working in her poolside garden all morning and afternoon, going at things with a relentless sense of focus, like you and your mother. If I hadn't asked her about lunch, she'd probably have worked straight through without a break. A perfect day for gardening, the first one since I arrived in Florida that's not only been sunny, but also mild and a little breezy, without a hint of humidity. Perfection, just a day before I'm scheduled to leave. But that's not the point of this little report. It's more about her and you, and how I keep seeing bits and pieces of you in her. Like the widow's peak from your father, the firmly set jaw from your mother, the deep-set eyes (origin unknown), the protruding ears from your maternal great-grandmother, the long, long legs, the diminutive fingers — so many resemblances that I keep wishing there were more, enough to make her your identical twin. Or nearly so. And then what? Incest? See how the mind works in search of its heart's desire?

But then again, I should also report that at dinner this evening, the joyousness of the occasion (and the transience of joy) made me feel I should advise Martha and Lynn to write their wills as soon as possible, with credit to you for having pushed us to do so. You, after all, inherited your father's hard-nosed sense of financial and legal affairs, whereas Martha got your mother's inability to cope with such things, as she suddenly realized last night. Who knows what accounts for such differences, but when all is said and done they make all the difference.

TUESDAY, MARCH 11
Dear Kate,

I had a puzzling dream last night that Martha helped me understand while we were at the airport this afternoon, waiting for my flight to Chicago. It began with a bird's-eye view of a house that you and I were having built within the bare walls of an already existing house. Looking down at the first day's work, I saw that the crew had framed in all the rooms on the ground floor, but they'd wasted some space in the right front corner of the house. So I told you about the problem and suggested that we ask the foreman to correct it. The next scene began with me telling him that you would oversee the project for us, but that I wanted to tell him about the unused space. "Just get on with it," you said. "But I want him to know that you're in charge of the project" was my immediate reply. And no sooner did I say that than the scene shifted again, this time to the exterior of the three-story house, where the foreman was suddenly falling head first from an upstairs window into a large trashcan. A nosedive of sorts that left me shocked and speechless, and that's when the dream ended.

When I told Martha about it, her first reaction was mock befuddlement: "What did you have for dinner?" But then she went on to suggest that the image of a house within the house might have come from Lynda's story about her colleague building a house within a barn. And I thought that the sudden disappearance of the foreman might be an analogue for your sudden death. But I still couldn't put the whole thing together until Martha said that "the house within the house might be the new home, the new life, that you're having to make for yourself in the old Victorian house that you and Kate used to live in together." The minute she said that, I realized the dream was telling me that I'll have to do it on my own, without the help of you or anyone else. "That," Martha said, "is why she was telling you to 'get on with it.'" Especially now that I'm returning to Iowa City.

WEDNESDAY, MARCH 12

Dear Kate,

For the first time in thirty-five years, you weren't there last night to meet me at the airport.

I knew, of course, that you wouldn't be, but that didn't make it any easier. Even before the plane landed, during the last few minutes of the descent, I began to feel so uneasy about it that I tried to distract myself by making a list of groceries to get on the way home. Walking out of the airplane and down the exit ramp toward the lobby, I told myself not to panic and it helped me to keep from choking up, but the minute I stepped on the escalator right before the lobby, a wave of shivers swept over me, like an echo of that first afternoon. Isn't it ridiculous that I can't control myself any better than that? It may sound crazy, but it's almost as if I'm programmed to react like that in any place or situation that triggers an acute sense of your absence. Driving home last night, I thought the chills would sweep over me again at the back door, but I was distracted by all the to and fro of carrying in my bags, putting away the groceries, sniffing the lilies of the valley that I planted on Valentine's Day, now fully in bloom, their sweet smell wafting through the house. Today, though, it happened again when I was sorting the accumulated mail myself for the first time in thirty-five years. Doing the chore you always chose to do, and there you were again, standing beside me at the dining room table, separating the ads from the bills from the letters from the magazines from the catalogs, reminding me as always not to open anything until everything is sorted. And as always I heeded your command, shivering from start to finish.

THURSDAY, MARCH 13
Dear Kate,

Terry called this morning to report that he received an e-mail and phone call last week about the potential fire hazards of Linda's nightly displays. I could hardly believe that anyone would be so worried as to contact the city parks director. Terry must have felt uneasy about having to call, for he started off with an apology. But who else could he call? Now that you're gone, I'm the only "contact person" for the neighborhood. He mentioned having noticed the candles a few months ago and surmised that they might be a memorial for you, but I guess he must have been surprised that it's still going on, since he asked if I knew anything about it. So I told him about Linda and how other people in the neighborhood have been making anonymous donations of candles to help share the cost of her project. And he in turn told me that one of the neighbors had spoken of city ordinances specifically outlawing untended fires. That's when I almost lost my cool. But I calmly replied that a few votive lights in the snow or the grass could hardly be considered a fire in the ordinary sense of the word. And so it went, congenial on both sides, the upshot being that I offered to talk with Linda about confining the candles to a safe spot in the park, and he offered to consult the city regulations to see if there might be allowance for a few memorial lights. But I'm uneasy about even mentioning the problem to Linda, since it's been such a labor of love on her part and a great gift to the neighorhood, even granting a few dissenters. In other words, I don't want to hurt her feelings or offend her in any way, and I certainly don't want to rouse her ire against Terry, since he's always been so helpful with the park. In other words, it's a complicated little situation that calls for your delicate sense of tact.

FRIDAY, MARCH 14
Dear Kate,

Terry called again this morning to report that the chief of police had just sent him a memo, noting that "an anonymous complaint was received yesterday evening about candles burning in Reno Street Park and an officer was dispatched to put out the candles." The chief also told Terry that city regulations prohibit candles or any other kind of unattended fire on city property. Isn't it weird — that a few candles could become such a big deal? Terry offered to call Linda and give her the bad news, but I thought it best for me to do so. And it's a good thing that I did, for her first reaction was as paranoid as mine, but gradually she came around to seeing that it was probably just a worrywart, unduly concerned about the risk of a fire. But that didn't dissuade her from "having some more fun," and sure enough there were three candles in the park this evening, and a row of eight more along the edge of Brad's property. Maybe I'll put a votive light in the old lamppost at the front of our property. Anything to keep the flame going.

I also spent part of this morning typing up some of your poems and sorting through snapshots for a booklet — a keepsake — that I plan to distribute at the service in May. And this afternoon, I took all the stuff to Sara, a designer at the university press, who's agreed to do the booklet on a freelance basis. "She'd want something very tasteful and low-key" is the way I began, "so I don't plan to write a big puff piece. She didn't like to blow her own horn, and didn't like me doing that sort of thing either." After listening to me talk about you and the booklet, Sara asked such thoughtful and careful questions that I'm sure she'll do a splendid job. So don't worry about it being mushy or sentimental.

On my way home from the press, I stopped at the co-op for some fresh fish and ran into my former student Emmy, who told me — I could hardly believe my good luck! — that she had a tape of your voice from the time that you gave her a tour of the trees in Hickory Hill. All the way home, I was in midair at the prospect of hearing you again. The only problem is that she called a while later, her voice so crestfallen that I immediately knew what was up — she had erased your voice in the process of using the tape for something else. Erased — just like that — and no way of bringing it back. How many times, in how many ways, am I going to lose you? No wonder I'm making a keepsake.

SUNDAY, MARCH 16
Dear Kate,

Now that Sara's at work on the booklet, I've been trying to get my head around everything else for the service. All of which makes me wonder how people arrange such things in the wake of a loved one's

death. I certainly couldn't have done it last November, given the shock
I was in back then. When I told that to Carolyn at the funeral home,
she said I was doing the right thing — that she often wished others
would put it off, but "most people just want to get it done and over
with." As in fast food, quick grief, over and out. Even if I hadn't been
a zombie, it would have been out of the question to have a service in
the grove, it was so bitterly cold right after you died. Better by far to be
celebrating your life on a balmy day when the trees you planted will be
fully in leaf — and people can share memories at a leisurely pace. I've
already called David, who'll talk about your poetry, and Jean, who'll
probably focus on your interior design, given the glass cases you did
for her and Jix. And I plan to contact Gert, since she was in on all your
tree projects. But that's just a start. I also hope to find someone other
than a minister who can serve as a master of ceremonies, not only to
introduce the program and the speakers, but also to conclude things,
say, with a recitation of the Lord's Prayer and the singing of "America
the Beautiful," which I remember as being your favorites. And I plan
to hire a flutist to offer a little prelude of pieces by Bach, in memory
of your flute-playing days and your devotion to the master. In other
words, something that's beautiful and tasteful from start to finish.
That's what I've been thinking about the past two days.

But who can I get to provide seating in the grove? And how can I
get an audio system without any source of power in the grove? And
how about a caterer for drinks and petits fours after the service? Or
would you rather I do that on the terrace? So many problems of staging and production that you could solve far better than I. Speaking of
which, I thought about reading something at the service but figured
you wouldn't approve. So I've decided to include something in the
booklet from *My Vegetable Love*, like the entry that deals with our wedding anniversary, when you took me to task for lamenting the drought-
ridden flowers from your perennial bed. "These are the flowers we
have," you said. "We don't have the others. So there's no point in talking about them." A maxim, I thought, for all seasons, especially now
that you're gone.

WEDNESDAY, MARCH 19

Dear Kate,

Last night I grilled a couple of beef tenderloins for me and my former student Kate. Like you, she's an unapologetic lover of steak, so I told her your maxim about meat-eaters and vegetarians — "Man is an omnivore, not an herbivore" — and she replied with a few mocking remarks of her own about the solemnity of her fish-eating friends. Well, as you can see, we had an agreeable dinner that I put together as carefully as you'd have done, complete with candles, flowers, linen napkins, hors d'oeuvres, wines, and a dessert. Also, of course, a few vegetables, like baked potatoes, steamed broccoli, and sliced tomatoes. And the conversation flowed easily — from Bush's impending war to Puck's good behavior to *The Hours* to her mother's sudden death and your sudden death to her collaborative work on Janusz's gulag memoir, to an editorial job she might take in Portland. And that's just a sample of what we talked about. Yet all the time she was here, I couldn't stop thinking of you — partly, of course, because of her name, also because she's as angular and youthful and sometimes as edgy as you were when we first met, also, no doubt, because I offered her some of your slacks and they fit her perfectly. Ultimately, though, I think that what got me was the totality of dinner itself, with her sitting across the table from me, just as you always did. Dinnertime, after all, remains one of the most emotionally loaded times of my day, if only because it was one of the most constant and sacred times of our marriage. This evening, for example, I was supposed to have dinner with David, but he called at five thirty, to call it off, given the onset of a cold so bad I could hardly recognize his voice. I sympathized with his distress, but no sooner did he hang up than I felt a strange sense of relief, despite having looked forward to a salmon dinner with him just a few minutes before — I'd even chilled a bottle of wine and bought some ingredients for a salad that I intended to bring. Yet the thought of staying home and putting together a meal for myself suddenly seemed preferable, and not just because the weather had suddenly turned raw. No, what it comes down to is that I have mixed feelings about dining in or dining out with anyone else but you. Which means that I'm often most comfortable when dining with Puck by my feet and a book or magazine by my side. Then, believe it or not, I don't miss you as much, except when I miss you more than you can possibly imagine.

THURSDAY, MARCH 20

Dear Kate,

The news of the day is war. Or as Bush preferred to put it last night on TV, we "are in the early stages of military operations to disarm Iraq, to free its people, and to defend the world from grave danger." How's that for an exercise in propaganda? As if to match Bush's garp with his own, Saddam Hussein (or perhaps a Saddam look-alike) appeared on television to assure the Iraqis that "you will be able to achieve glory and your despicable infidel enemies will be defeated." Exactly what's happening is hard to tell, because our missile and airplane attack on Baghdad began at four in the morning Iraq time, supposedly aimed at "targets of opportunity" (i.e., buildings or bunkers where Saddam Hussein and his sons might have been hiding, according to "advance intelligence reports"). And now, almost twenty hours later, no one in an official capacity is prepared to say whether our strike was success- ful or even if the Iraqi person on TV was Saddam or a Saddam wannabe. The only thing that's clear is that we've acted in violation of international law — making war upon another nation without having been attacked by them ourselves. So even Walter Cronkite has spoken out against our worldwide loss of credibility.

Given how closely you followed such things on TV, I stayed up un- til one thirty this morning, switching from channel to channel, to get every bit of information. But no matter which channel I watched, the only thing I could see was a fuzzy picture of Baghdad, a minaret in the background, with voice-over commentary about the "surgical strike," the "surprise attack," the "bunker-busters," the "packages," all aimed at "targets of opportunity." Such boring and repetitious news that bed seemed far more appealing, especially given the possibility of a dream. And sure enough, you made a memorable appearance, starting with a little scene at home, just when we were leaving for Adagio. You were in the kitchen, chiding me for being late, while I was in the living room, telling you that "I only have to put on my shoes and socks, so just go ahead and wait for me in the car. I'll be right out." Isn't it strange that I was fully dressed — pants, shirt, tie, sport jacket and all, but still hadn't put on my shoes and socks. Sounds like I was dragging my feet, seeing as how I put my shoes on before my socks, and then had to take them off and start all over again, while you were still in the kitchen, more and more impatient, telling me over and over again that "we're late for our reservation." Then the scene switched, and I was seated at our restaurant table, but you, oddly enough, were crouching under the table, and gradually emerged head first, your hair dyed completely blond with bangs coming down almost to your eyebrows. Such a striking transformation of your brown hair that I was momentarily speechless, but then said, "You look beautiful, just beautiful." At which point you suddenly went spinning out of your chair and wound up sprawling face down on the floor. I, in turn, quickly ran over to help, but you said, "It's nothing really, I just spun out of my chair." And then I awoke, marveling at how imaginatively and ingeniously my dream had condensed what we went through the night and noon before your died. A reminder, as if I needed one, of the film that's been playing in my head, again and again, ever since that afternoon.

FRIDAY, MARCH 21
Dear Kate,

Karl called this morning to report that the blood test I had on Wednesday indicates that my thyroid supplement needs a little boost. Thirty-five years ago — fit, trim, and newly married to you — it never occurred to me that I might have a wonky thyroid, but now my bulging middle and aching knees are as sure a proof as a blood test. Also my dozing off last night at nine thirty. But my problems are nothing compared to my brother's, judging from his phone call this afternoon. He sounded quite good at first, but then told me about a worrisome episode last weekend, when his eyesight temporarily went bad — "defective" is the way he put it — and words failed him when he tried to explain the problem to Phyllis. So, he's wondering whether he should still try to give a few talks that he's scheduled for this spring and summer. And should he fly to Italy for a month, as planned? Though he asked my opinion and I advised him against anything that might risk his life (or the quality of his life), he seemed to be more touched by my allusion to your sudden death than by any wisdom it might contain for the rest of his life. What is it, I wonder, that impels him to sally forth again and again, even in the face of his drastically failing powers? Is that what Thomas meant by his commandment — "Do not go gentle into that good night"? And if that's the case, what should I be doing?

Trudy called this afternoon to report that she's back in Wyoming again, gradually getting acclimated to life at nine thousand feet above sea level. Though you and I never got adjusted to the thin air, the vistas from there were so splendid they make me wish I had a mountain in the backyard or something to climb so I can see what it looks like from up there. Or maybe I should just start a few lettuce and broccoli seeds, so I'm ready when the ground warms up. Tending my gardens and yours will probably be a steep enough climb for me.

SATURDAY, MARCH 22

Dear Kate,

Can you imagine how you'd answer an interviewer who asked a question like this: "I'd like you to talk a bit, if you will, about how creativity figures not only in your writing, but also in your gardening, and other aspects of your life." That's how things began when a fellow named Lin came to interview me this morning for a profile in one of the university's promotional magazines. Such a huge and abstract question that I was stymied at first, until I remembered the day you put a brick border around my vegetable garden and inspired me to think of it as a three-dimensional picture. And then I remembered the Christmas you gave me the large cloth-bound journal for keeping a diary of my garden. And then your ingenious suggestions during the year of *My Vegetable Love* — like the time you said, "Let's go to the Monet exhibit in Chicago, so you can write about his waterlilies and ours." And then your daily reactions to my journal entries, as in, "That's not what I said" or "That's not exactly what happened" or "That's not quite the right wording." Words that put such a high premium on getting things right that they inspired me to write as carefully as I could from start to finish. Others, I realize, might wither under such reactions, but for me they were a gift you never stopped giving. No wonder it's sometimes very hard to write you these letters — another diary of sorts — without your critiques to guide me.

Speaking of critiques, I wonder how you'd respond to the letter I received this afternoon from Vassar's associate director for donor relations, who began by asking me to "please accept my condolences in addition to those you have already received on the death of your wife." Altogether, it seemed a bit chilly, also somewhat ill worded, since I don't think one receives "condolences . . . on" something. But perhaps

I'm being Miss Fidget, worrying about the wording when perhaps I should be wondering about the motive of someone in her position sending me the recent issue of the *Vassar Quarterly* that lists your name on page sixty-four. On the other hand, I was surprised and touched by an e-mail I received yesterday from Marcia, reporting a very generous gift from the University of Iowa Foundation to your memorial fund. There's more than one way to skin a cat, which makes me wonder how Stanford will respond when they get the news of your death.

SUNDAY, MARCH 23
Dear Kate,

Today was so sunny and warm that I planted my first vegetable seeds outside — radishes and peas — a week or two earlier than usual. When I ran my fingers through the soil, it felt so good that I wanted to tell you about it then and there. The only problem is that I wonder what I'll do with all the radishes — two hundred or more for me, my-self, and I. Maybe they'll come on gradually enough that I can savor them all spring. As for the legumes, I was contemplating a bumper crop of snow peas, when your plaintive request of years ago suddenly came to mind, "Aren't you going to plant some shell peas too? They're so sweet and tender, and you can't ever get them in the store." And I remembered my churlish response — "So few peas for so much space and so much fuss, it hardly makes sense." But of course I couldn't re-fuse you back then and still couldn't today. And not just because they're so sweet and tender, but also because I was touched by your childhood memory of shelling peas on your grandmother's back porch. Then, of course, I remembered you shelling them on our back porch. And now, it seems I'm destined to be shelling them there myself.

THURSDAY, MARCH 27
Dear Kate,

Jo Ann called this morning from Barrington, to confirm that she and Bob will be visiting next month and to talk about things in the gar-den, which led her to ask if you had a fondness for pussy willows. "Fondness," I told her, "is an understatement. Kate wrote a poem about cutting and forcing them in early spring. I'll send you a copy. It's called 'Early Gardening.'" After talking to Jo Ann, I checked on your pussy willow and discovered that it's just right for cutting. So I pruned several branches, with an eye to putting them in the corner of the living room — peeling two or three inches of bark off the bottom of each, pounding the debarked portions with a hammer, then arranging them spraylike in a vase, just as you always did. Your earliest springtime ritual. The only problem was that your ashes are in that corner in your grandmother's black vase, and there isn't any other place in the living room that would be suitable for the catkins. So I put them on top of the dining-room plant stand, and there they stand in tribute to the season, to you, and the wisdom of your poem — that "where we kill the bare stem will multiply."

FRIDAY, MARCH 28

Dear Kate,

The weather turned colder last night, so it was a good day for answering a bunch of e-mail and writing some thank-you notes for gifts to your memorial fund. Most of the notes were easy to do, until I was writing your cousin Mary, telling her about my plans to scatter your ashes in Hanalei Bay. Just then, without thinking, I looked up from the dining room table, looked over at the sideboard, saw the picture of you walking along the Kalalau Trail, as if you were about to walk off the edge of the world right into the blue, blue sky. And suddenly I was in tears. Which makes me think I'm still more vulnerable than I imagined — liable to be unstrung by almost anything that suddenly takes me back. Back to our lives together in Hawaii, in the backyard, in the kitchen, at the dining room table, in bed, in the Jeep. You name it. So many spots in time, so many time bombs, it's a wonder that I'm not exploding more often, morning, noon, and night. But in truth, I'm not crying as much as before. Sometimes, in fact, I go two or three days without choking up, as I did this week until today. In other words, something is taking its course, though I don't know how to describe it, except to say that I seem to have moved beyond the intense grief of the last few months into something that feels more like an overwhelming sense of sadness for you, for me, for Puck and Jag, for all that we've lost and all that we had when you were still alive. Some-

times the feeling is so generalized that it's more like a brooding awareness of things, rather than the sharp pang of a specific memory such
as our hike along the Kalalau Trail that glittering afternoon, when you
spurred us on with your irrepressible sense of time — "If we don't do
this now, we might never do it again." I worry sometimes that I might
regain so much of my composure that I'll be able to think of you or remember you without a twinge. But all I need is a little episode like this
afternoon to remind me that I'm not unflappable and probably never
will be.

WEDNESDAY, APRIL 2
Dear Kate,

A year ago today, as I discovered from working on our income
taxes, we drove to the leeward side of Maui right after lunch, because
you wanted to see Lahaina, that tourist trap I'd been avoiding for
twenty years. "It's always best," you said, "to see how the enemy lives."
But the weather there was so hot that no sooner did we leave the central valley and start driving north along the coast than you were fretting about the heat (and so was I). And not even a midafternoon drink
overlooking the harbor was enough to cool us down, nor the shade of
the blockwide banyan tree next door. But it sure did make for a memorable spot. I thought of that tree this morning, sitting under an oak
by the Cedar River in Sutliff, where I took Carol to show her the beguiling spot you first showed me some thirty-six years ago. A long way
from Lahaina, and a better place to beat the heat, thanks to a gentle
breeze, the glistening river, the iron bridge, a few fishermen floating
by, and a well-chilled bottle of wine. Carol was so enchanted that she
burst into song, "Heaven, I'm in heaven," and imagined Fred Astaire
dancing along the riverbank with Ginger Rogers. I preferred Audrey
Hepburn, and Carol readily agreed to the change. Something about
Hepburn must have taken us back — maybe because she came of age
when we did — for Carol was soon sharing memories of Pierre, and I
of you, there by the riverside of your childhood. Too bad the bridge
was closed, so I couldn't show her how the century-old planks clattered under our wheels, clattered every time as if they might give way,
wheel-upon-wood-upon-wheel-upon-wood.

SATURDAY, APRIL 5

Dear Kate,

Linda's gone legal and put solar lights on top of the park sign and on top of the kiosk. But last night she had a little rebellion with another big candle display. I wonder what other surprises she has in store. As for me, there's nothing much to report the past few days, except that it looks like I need to go on a diet — as soon as possible. How else to explain the dream I had last night? We were in bed together, fondling each other, staring and smiling at each other, when you looked down at my stomach and suddenly pulled away in disgust. "How can you let yourself get like that, when I'm doing everything I can to keep you alive?" A familiar refrain from years past when I was eating my way through this or that crisis, but never so grossly as now. "The great rotundity," as you used to call it, is greater than ever before. So, for breakfast this morning, I forsook my English muffin and confined myself to shredded wheat with three sliced strawberries and 1 percent acidophilus milk. For lunch, I cut the bread as thinly as possible and made myself only one sandwich, with one slice of roast beef, slivered onions, cucumbers, tomatoes, and lettuce, and just a dab of lite mayonnaise. But at a dinner party this evening, I could hardly refuse the purée of pea soup with a dollop of sour cream, or the roast pork tenderloin with a wild rice–brown rice casserole, laced with spinach and cheese, or the pinot noir, or the piquant salad of mixed greens with minced oranges and a citrus vinaigrette, or the sauvignon blanc, or the raspberry sherbet with sliced mangoes and blackberries, or the Grand Marnier? No wonder I stumbled home, fearful of another guilt-ridden dream. But it sure was a pleasure to break bread with others, except when someone asked if I'm working on a new book, and I mentioned these letters and the problem of writing without the guidance of my in-house critic, but Carol quickly assured me that "she's right there inside your head." And I could hardly disagree, though I sure wish there were a better way to keep in touch. The mind's a fine and private place, but none I think do there embrace.

SUNDAY, APRIL 6

Dear Kate,

Last night, you were there again in my dreams, but not, thank God, to reprove me. No, this time, you returned from the dead announcing that you were back for five days. A brief reprieve. A taste of life after death. So how did we spend that precious time? Doing something special? Taking one of the trips we planned — to the Galapagos, to Australia, or northern Italy? Rolling all our pleasures into one last splurge? Au contraire, we did the things we usually do this time of year, clearing the refuse off your perennial bed, pruning the grapes, raking the lawn, cleaning up the park. And hanging out around the house — reading, watching TV, cooking and eating our nightly meals. As if our days would never end. How strange, I thought, after waking up, but then I remembered how we spent the week before you died, raking leaves, planting daffodils, cleaning house, getting ready for Gene's visit. Now, come to think of it, I can hardly imagine a better way to spend one's final days than savoring the ordinary pleasures of life. That's what I did most of today, breakfasting a bit later than usual, thanks to the time change, making my way through the Sunday paper, transplanting the arugula and mei qing choi, checking the copy-edited manuscript for the textbook, moving the newly germinated pepper seedlings up to the grow lights, putting clean sheets on the bed. An ordinary day around the house, except for an extraordinary spurt of hot water when I drained the air from the living room radiator. Like the spurt back in January. But this time, I moved quickly enough to put my finger over the spout, bend over and find the little stopper on the floor, my finger still over the spout, then remove my finger and screw the stopper in fast enough to prevent the spout from spraying the love-seat. That's more or less how I'm feeling these days — that I can get through this vale of tears if I just keep my finger over the spout.

TUESDAY, APRIL 8

Dear Kate,

The garlics and daffodils are up to their tips in snow. And the radishes — what must it be like for them, suffocating under the weight of their snow-laden row covers? So much for "a beautiful overnight storm." If you were here, I'd be fretting even more, and you'd be reminding me that every year I "worry things to death, and every year they survive. Just wait and see." So I'm trying to learn a little patience. Now if I can also develop a taste for the absurd, I'll be ready for anything that comes, including frost-bitten garlic and freeze-dried daffodils. I was musing on the absurdity of things during my checkup this afternoon, when Karl was thumping my knees, peering into my eyes, checking my reflexes for signs of neurological trouble, and my thoughts veered inexorably to the emergency room doctor checking your reflexes, all of them so far gone you could barely move your head when he asked if you could hear him. And suddenly I couldn't help wondering what difference it makes whether I can shrug my shoulders, bare my teeth, squeeze his fingers, or do any of the other things that might prove my neurological fitness. Why bother, when the only fingers that I care to squeeze are gone? And the same goes for shrugging my shoulders and baring my teeth. Why bother, if you're not here to behold the grimace?

A few days ago, Trudy called from Wyoming, back in her cabin for the first time in two years — a happy return, I thought. But her Rocky Mountain high has turned out to be a downer — far from the solace she thought it would be when her father and mother were dying. Maybe it could never have been commensurate with her yearnings to be there again. But I also think that her parents' deaths were bound to change her view of the place, and not just because it's no longer a getaway, but because death, after all, has a way of putting everything in its place, even the things we cherish. I certainly felt that way when I was transplanting the broccoli and cauliflower today — such vigorous seedlings, they look like emblems of spring, of life reborn, but life without you seems like spring without rain.

WEDNESDAY, APRIL 9

Dear Kate,

Trish is in town for a week, as a visiting writer in the nonfiction program, and she's here just five days after her mother died — two days after a full-blown funeral mass and an Irish wake to boot. She must be going on nerves alone, but whatever it is, I feel like a sluggard by comparison — also like I'm suffering from amnesia. At lunch, she asked me to suggest some essayists for a nonfiction course she's teaching next fall, but I could hardly get the names out. And it wasn't any better when I was trying to bring her up to date on the nonfiction list that we're co-editing for Holly. And it was the same with memories of you. She remembered things I'd completely forgotten — like the picnic where you brought a poached turkey breast and then taught her how to do it and also how to make a light mayonnaise with the gizmo that you got from your mother. And no sooner were we done with lunch than she hustled off to get ready for her workshop later this afternoon, whereas I drove home to rest up before dinner at David's.

At David's, I had another disarming encounter, this time with Towhe, a former student from Nigeria, back for the first time in twenty years, but remembering things as vividly as if they'd taken place yesterday or the day before. Yet it wasn't his memory that disarmed me so much as his strange counsel, urging me to stop thinking about you, though he had no way of knowing how much you've been on my mind — advising me also to turn your image toward the wall, though again he couldn't have known how much I've been dwelling on pictures of you, except, perhaps, for his familiarity with grieving Americans. But above all he implored me to study yoga, so my "spirit" might be liberated to heal itself and me. Given such a radically different view of things, can you imagine how chagrined he was to discover that I'm writing you these letters? Though I couldn't imagine myself taking his counsel, I certainly did wish that I too could attain such peace of mind as he seems to possess, especially when I discovered we're the very same age. But I wonder if he'd be so tranquil had he ever been married, ever been in love, and suddenly lost the love of his life. Then perhaps he might understand why it's not enough for me to keep telling myself that "I'm getting better, I'm getting better, I'm getting better," as if I were the little engine that could.

FRIDAY, APRIL 11

Dear Kate,

Yesterday I got so involved in finishing the tax forms, then putting on a dinner for Trish, that I didn't have time to write anything before going to bed last night. So this is a two-day report, inspired by the loveliest weather this spring — clear skies, gentle breezes, temperatures in the sixties and seventies. All the snow suddenly gone and everything much greener — the garlics and daffodils as buoyant as you always said they'd be. Everything more colorful too. The aconites, snow-drops, squills, and crocuses fully on display. The miniature iris you planted last fall suddenly in bloom at the edge of the terrace. No won-der Trish was transfixed by the yard (and the feeling of your presence). Which made me wonder how you could possibly have forsaken all of this for a trip to Hawaii? When I looked at the calendar yesterday morning, and remembered we were supposed to be winging our way to the mid-Pacific just then, I also wondered what you'd have done about all the remaining plants to be moved to your new perennial bed. How could you have turned your back on two years of work that you and I nearly finished last fall? Thanks to Chris it was all finished today. He arrived early this morning at eight thirty and worked almost non-stop until late this afternoon, digging and transplanting, digging and transplanting. But before his work could begin, he and I walked around the bed for almost two hours, eyeballing all the dried leavings of last fall, first to identify the plants yet to be moved, then to imagine exactly where you'd have put them. In the middle of that exercise, I felt your absence so keenly I could barely contain myself. But the design of your new bed, its elaborate patterns and repetitions visible even now, en-abled us to figure things out as if guided by you.

TUESDAY, APRIL 15
Dear Kate,

Here it is four days since I last wrote, four days so warm that I was sweating, even in shorts and a t-shirt. Maybe it wouldn't have been op-pressive if I'd just been sitting at the kitchen table in the cool of the evening, as I am right now, writing you a late-night letter. But instead I was on a frantic countdown, getting things ready for Bob and Jo Ann — and not just for their visit but also for the dinner party that I put on this evening, just a few hours after they arrived. A sit-down af-fair for ten, with hors d'oeuvres on the terrace. Yes, I know you'd have dressed me down for scheduling a dinner party on the same night as their arrival. But I had no choice, given that they're dining at Grinnell the next three days while Bob is a guest lecturer. So, the past few days, I've been bopping back and forth between things for their visit and things for the dinner. Flowers for their room, flowers for the living room, the dining room table, and the terrace. Clean sheets and towels for them, a clean set of linen napkins and placemats for the table. Orange juice, freshly ground coffee, cream, croissants, and English muffins for their breakfast; white wine, red wine, mineral water, dessert wine, paté, goat cheese, kalamata olives, crackers, leg of lamb, new potatoes, scallions, parsley, asparagus, fresh tomatoes, oranges, kiwi fruit, and romaine for the dinner party. Also leaves and chairs for the dining room table, as well as tables and chairs for the terrace. Now I know why you went batty whenever we had houseguests — and you didn't have to do it alone. Nor did you have to clean up the terrace, tidy up the fish pond, recycle the trash, take Puck to the vet's, and do lunch with Trish and Holly in the middle of today's preparations — and then after lunch come home to set the table and start preparing the meal, only to discover that Bob and Jo Ann had arrived three hours earlier than expected and were waiting on the terrace. No wonder I suddenly felt like the lead character in a new play called *Get the Host!* But Jo Ann was so helpful that together we got everything done just before the guests arrived. The only problem is that I mistakenly set the table for eight rather than ten, and only realized the error when I counted six of us on the terrace with four more yet to come. And again Jo Ann saved the day, suggesting that we put two people at each end of the table rather than one, that we pull in two additional chairs from the terrace — and lo! the table was fully reset, your Thai silk runner down the center of it, without any sign of a mishap. But how to explain the applause that erupted not once but twice during dinner? Maybe it was the wine. Maybe it was the food, all of it as vivid and tasty as spring itself, especially the lamb — "It's so tender, so perfectly cooked! Where did you get it? How did you do it?" Maybe it was also a tribute to you, everything so inspired by your vision of things — "the gospel according to Kate" — that your spirit was manifest.

WEDNESDAY, APRIL 16
Dear Kate,

Bob and Jo Ann went to Grinnell for the afternoon and early evening, but before they left she spent the morning in your perennial bed, weeding, cutting back the fall refuse, clearing away the detritus. Such a painstaking act of friendship that it was touching to see her in the bed,

Jag running back and forth as always when you were there. I wanted to join in, but it seemed as if she was intent on communing with you and your plants. I think she might also have been inspired by the picture of you in the middle of the bed that I sent her a few weeks ago — "I just love it, I just love that picture of her with her arms spread out above all those flowers." While Jo Ann was tending your garden, Bob told me a bit of what he went through when Joan died some thirty years ago, and I was fascinated to hear him speak so frankly of his grief and lone-liness — "I was still a young man, still in my early forties, and I didn't want to spend the rest of my life alone. Joan knew that I hoped to marry again, and encouraged me to do it, but that's because we had a long time to talk about things before she died." How different it was for you and me! You went so swiftly, without warning, that there wasn't even a minute for us to talk. And given my age, there really isn't time for me to start a new life, even if I wanted one. When I told that to Bob, he paused for a moment, mulling the possibilities. "Well, I suppose it's less likely for you than it was for me, but you never can tell what might happen." What I couldn't explain to him just then was that it's out of the question, that I've closed the valves of my attention, that I only have eyes for you.

Before going to Grinnell, Bob also shepherded me through the mysteries of buying and installing a DVD player, which I've been thinking about ever since Amy said you'd been planning to give me one for Christmas. Now, thanks to Bob (and the DVD subtitles), I can see a movie and follow the dialogue, as I discovered this evening by watching *Far from Heaven*, every scene of which, every word of which bears witness to such a hapless marriage that it made me keenly aware of how lucky we were.

FRIDAY, APRIL 18
Dear Kate,

Today was a hard one — more painful than any the past few weeks. In part, I think it's Bob and Jo Ann, so in sync that I feel like an odd man out, a spectator of love, a voyeur of sorts, witnessing them and re-membering all that we've lost. And to make matters worse, this morn-ing I showed them some pictures of you and me, pictures they were eager to see, but that only made me more intensely conscious of our special times together — in the garden, in the kitchen, in the park, in San Francisco, in Shanghai. The same thing happened when I showed Jo Ann your handmade clothes — your muumuus reminded me of our times in Hawaii, where we're supposed to be right now. And then during lunch, I found myself listening to them talk about plays we'll never see together and places we'll never go together. By the time they went to Grinnell this afternoon, I was so upset that I broke down in tears, but now, as I sit here after dinner, contemplating this day and others past, I'm more at peace with things, thanks to being alone once again, thanks also to making a stew, as you would, from the leftover lamb. Eating my way through grief again and sopping it up with bread. What else to do on Good Friday?

SATURDAY, APRIL 19

Dear Kate,

Here it is the day before Easter, and for the first time in thirty-five years I didn't spend the afternoon putting together a basket to put by your side of the bed before you wake up tomorrow. So come morning, I won't hear you calling out, "Oh, look, come look and see what the Easter bunny brought me!" Far from getting goodies for you, I spent this morning with Bob buying a bonbon for myself — a new twenty-four-inch TV with a flat screen and stereo sound. I never imagined myself owning such a thing, because I hardly watch TV. But Bob was so convincing, I couldn't resist: "Now that you've got a new DVD, you need a new TV to go with it, so let's go spend some more of your new-found wealth. You won't believe how much better it looks and sounds than this antique of yours." And it's true, the picture is so large and vivid, the color so striking, that I could see the actors' faces more clearly than ever before, wrinkles and all. A good thing to see, for the movie we watched this afternoon, *Last Orders*, was about the death of an aging British butcher, played by Michael Caine, and the seriocomic way that his long-time friends and his adopted son come to terms with his demise on their way to scattering his ashes at Margate Pier. Bob's been wanting me to rent it ever since he arrived, and now I know why, seeing as how it bears witness to the power of memory, bringing the butcher to life again through the vivid recollections of his friends. In the middle of the movie, I was suddenly in tears, remembering our earliest days together as I watched the youthful encounters of the butcher and his wife, played by your favorite, Helen Mirren. And at the end of the movie, Bob was in tears, remembering, I imagine, the day when he scattered Joan's ashes in the waters off Providence.

SUNDAY, APRIL 20

Dear Kate,

Easter Sunday, and I thought it would be a non-event, especially after Bob and Jo Ann left this morning, without waiting for breakfast. You know how it is when Bob sets his mind on something, and this morning he was hellbent on getting an early start. But the day picked up with a call from Hannah and the news that she's now beginning to work with grieving adults as well as children. So perhaps that's why she seemed more eager to hear me out than usual and assure me that my gloom will not be a permanent thing — "It's not surprising, Dad, that you're still in the valley and likely to be there awhile. But the clouds will lift, things will gradually change. Probably they're already changing, but maybe not enough for you to notice." Just then I heard a knock on the back door, and there was my former graduate student Becky together with a friend, biking in the neighborhood and come to pay me a visit.

After signing off with Hannah, I showed them around the yard, but gardening was suddenly in the background when I discovered that Becky's friend had lost her husband, just three years ago, as abruptly as I lost you. And worse still, he died on a business trip to Brazil, so they weren't even together when he died. No wonder she was in shock for a year. No wonder she asked if I'd been throwing things (I told her you'd never approve). No wonder she sometimes looked at me with such a piercing gaze I could hardly look back. No wonder she understood why I can't make sense of my life. "Of course you can't, because it doesn't make sense, and it won't until you're able to make sense of it anew." No wonder Becky brought her to visit and said almost nothing while the two of us talked, sharing our grief and a bottle of Chablis. Oh yes, we also talked about cooking together — you and me, she and her husband — and we talked about dining together. So when she and Becky were leaving, I gave her a copy of *My Vegetable Love*, and then she was gone, biking down the drive and out of my life as suddenly as she'd arrived.

MONDAY, APRIL 21

Dear Kate,

Why did you wake me up at five this morning? And then having roused me, why did you suddenly disappear? I was sleeping on my side, facing the bedroom wall, when I heard you calling my name, "Carl, Carl, Carl," as if you were desperate to get my attention. I rolled over and there you were, standing by your side of the bed, looming over me, taller, it seemed, by a foot or so, dressed in your blue and white house-coat. But no sooner did I see you than you suddenly disappeared — poof! Just a few tiny particles lingering in the air. A brief but stunning dream, which I thought might be the result of my talking about you yesterday with Becky and her friend, showing them pictures of you, telling them stories about you. But now I remember how you always nudged me awake or called me by name whenever I was moaning in my sleep. So perhaps that's what happened this morning — a night-mare and then you bringing me out of it. Better still, maybe it's an em-blem of things to come, or what's going on even now, without my knowing it until now. You bringing me out of it, day by day by day.

I wish there were someone or something that could do the same for Trudy, who called this afternoon to report that she's spending a couple of weeks in Missoula, not only to attend a wildlife film festival but also to recover from the altitude sickness that's been dogging her more and more at her cabin. It's gotten so bad that she might have to sell it, which I can hardly imagine, and not just because of its majestic vistas, or even because of its access to the wildlife that she studies and writes about. It's that she's married to the place, or, as she put it this after-noon, "It's the most important relationship in my life, the thing that's meant as much to me as a marriage or a longstanding relationship with someone else." An announcement that touched me more deeply than she might have imagined, given the thirty-two years that you and I lived together in this house of ours.

TUESDAY, APRIL 22

Dear Kate,

Ever since Bob told me about the year that Joan was dying of cancer, I've been wondering what it might have been like if you had died slowly rather than swiftly, gradually rather than suddenly. Bob, of course, is not the first person to make me ponder such a thing. I've thought about alternative scenarios ever since the day itself, when the fatuous neurologist tried to comfort me with the bromide that "it's better she's going like this than to linger on like a vegetable for twenty more years, like a friend of mine." The third time he offered me that sop, I wanted to strangle him with my bare hands, telling him that "it's better you're going like this" again and again. He wasn't the only one to offer me such pablum. Others have given me this bit of consolation — "At least she went so fast that she didn't know what was happening and didn't suffer any pain." Or this one — "Just think of how much worse it might have been if she had lingered on for several months." Whenever I hear that line, trite though it is, I can hardly ignore the horrific alternative, at least for a few fleeting seconds. But Bob's story made me think about a different alternative, the possibility of you dying gradually, losing touch slowly over several months, yet still sufficiently in command of your powers at first to be outraged by the injustice, as you surely would have been, especially after having survived the ordeal of breast cancer, but then taking such command of the situation as to put all your affairs in order, and mine as well, before a final trip to Hawaii, and then . . . The only problem, of course, is that I couldn't spell out the rest, except to imagine such a tender parting and a poignant dissolve, with Hanalei Bay in the background, that I knew the whole thing was preposterous. A Hollywood movie. *South Pacific: The Sequel.* Which reminded me again of what you said on the drought-ridden day of our thirtieth anniversary, when I was remembering the lovely bouquet you made for the day of our wedding: "These are the flowers that we have. We don't have the others, so there's no point in talking about them."

THURSDAY, APRIL 24

Dear Kate,

Just as predicted, the rain came overnight and lasted all day, a gentle soaker that settled the onion plants in so nicely I'm sure they'll take hold. Too bad it didn't go as well with the bio of you I've been writing for the memorial booklet — I finished drafting it yesterday afternoon when Sara called to tell me she needs it tomorrow. But Holly fussed over my draft so much that she trimmed all my echoes and emphases. When I got her revision in this morning's e-mail, I called right away, suggesting alternatives, like reducing the type size, or expanding the trim size, or dropping some of the snapshots, anything to make more room for my full-length bio. But then she told me that the type was already small, and the booklet would only include a handful of snapshots, which sent me into such a panic that I rushed over to the press for a preview of Sara's mockup, which was so elegantly simple that at first I too didn't want to change it at all. Yet I also wanted to make room for the full bio and a few other snapshots as well. No choice but to increase the booklet from twelve to sixteen pages and then ask Sara to make a new layout of the material and a new selection of snapshots within the newly increased length. After an hour of trying to rearrange things myself, I could see why Sara is designing it rather than me.

SUNDAY, APRIL 28

Dear Kate,

I overdid it the past two days, transplanting all the spring vegetables, overdid it so much I can barely move. But the pain in my joints is nothing like the ache in my head when I think about the absurdity of having planted so much stuff with only one of us left to eat it. This morning, for example, I put in twelve broccoli plants, twelve cauliflower plants, twelve napa cabbage seedlings, and twelve mei qing chois. Forty-eight crucifers for one person! And this afternoon, I put in thirteen romaine seedlings, twelve oak-leaf lettuce seedlings, nine arugula seedlings, and nine escarole seedlings — in other words, forty-three separate greens that will produce more pickings, more heads of things than I can possibly use before they bolt in the summer heat. I knew it was excessive, the minute I started planting. But I couldn't stop, couldn't cut back. Partly it was habit. Partly it was space — nature abhors a vacuum, and would fill it with weeds if I didn't fill it myself. But largely, I think, it was aesthetic — balancing rows of broccoli and cauliflower, salad greens and Asian greens, everything arranged to produce blocks of contrasting height, color, shape, and texture. The problem, of course, is that I'm the only one here to behold my elegant array of things, and even I can't see them without removing the protective row covers. In other words, life goes on here just as before — Carl the Compulsive planting his decoratively designed vegetable garden, then turning it into a field of row covers.

Better I should tell you that your beloved waxwings are back in the apple trees, drunk on blossoms. And that Linda put on a glittering show last night. And that Raeburn has agreed to preside at your memorial service. His chairmanly manner will assure a proper sense of ceremony, as will a flutist, who has agreed to perform the Bach *Partita for Unaccompanied Flute*. Now all that's left is to hire a caterer, type up the program, and confirm the funeral home's arrangements for audio, seating, and newspaper announcements. The more I think about all the details, the more it seems like I'm staging an open-air theater production. I just hope we get a decent turnout — and good weather.

TUESDAY, APRIL 29
Dear Kate,

Chris turned up with a truckload of dirt this morning to fill in your old perennial bed and seed it with grass. But no sooner did he get it leveled than a rain started to fall, and it's predicted to hang in for several days. So it looks like I'm housebound for awhile, and without any projects to pass the time of day, my mind got the better of me, and I soon found myself wondering how your grieving husband has been doing the past few weeks. Which led me to spend a few hours reading the letters I've written you this month. Narcissus at home, you might say, taking my pulse. But I discovered some interesting things. For example, despite what Eliot said, April is not the cruelest month, not by a long shot. Oh yes, I had some tearful days when Bob and Jo Ann were here, and some chills too, but otherwise I've been dry-eyed from start to finish. A notable improvement, especially when you consider that I was congratulating myself at the end of March just for going three days without crying. But I've not only been counting the days without this or that — I've also been looking at what I've been doing from day to day. Quality as well as quantity, and that's where April has really stood out from before. In the garden, with guests, with the nonfiction series, with plans for the memorial service — with a sense of possibility that I hadn't really felt until now. And I don't feel guilty about feeling that way, though I can't help wondering how to account for the change — whether it's the advent of spring, or the passage of time, or some internal compass, gradually reorienting itself without my even knowing it. As if there were something inside my head, laying down a new emotional network, or repairing the old one, or doing whatever is needed to help me adapt to a world without you. I've heard about psychologists doing research on the way people adjust to plea- surable or painful events, and the unnerving results suggest that our brains evidently regulate us, whether we know it or not, bringing us back to an emotional setpoint, a state of equilibrium that corrects our most ecstatic or despairing moods. Sounds creepy, like an innate sort of mood-altering system, but then again it's not half so creepy as my reading these letters to find out how I'm doing, as if I couldn't tell just from the fact that I'm still writing you these letters, still longing to be in touch. All of which is to say that at some level I'm adapting — or, as Beckett would say, "something is taking its course." But then again, I'm not adapting at all, or, as cummings would say, "the best gesture of my brain is less than your eyelids flutter."

WEDNESDAY, APRIL 30

Dear Kate,

Sara gave me her final proof for the memorial booklet this morn- ing, now expanded to sixteen pages, and the whole thing looks much better than before, thanks to the larger collection of snapshots. The front cover has your full name all in caps on three separate lines, first KATE, then FRANKS, then KLAUS, and below that a childhood pic- ture of you, probably age eight or nine, standing in front of your grand- mother's house with a buoyant smile on your face; the back cover has nothing on it but the color shot of you walking into the distance along the Na Pali coast in Kauai. The booklet itself contains eighteen more shots of you, interspersed with the biographical note, an excerpt from *My Vegetable Love*, and four of your poems, all set in an elegant Basker- ville type on a lovely cream-colored paper. I'm sure you'd consider it "a wretched excess" — but that's the sort of thing you always did for special occasions, so it seems only fitting that I should do the same for you.

Talking of special occasions, I watched a movie last night that in- spired me more than anything else I've recently seen. Called *Himalaya*, it's a story of generational struggle in a small Tibetan community dur- ing their annual trek across the mountains. But beyond the story of youth against age, it's a vivid depiction of the people and their yaks, pitted against the stark ferocity of the windswept mountains. In other words, a vision of human endurance and the importance of enduring, no matter how painful the challenge. I told Trudy about it when she called this morning, and she raved about it too. But her difficulties in the high mountain air continue to be so bad that endurance is not even a choice for her if she wants to survive. Sometimes I think I should be grateful just to be living here in reasonably good health in a bountiful place where the grief of living without you is not compounded by the struggle against anything else. The wind is still so fierce that it's all I can do just to keep my footing.

FRIDAY, MAY 2
Dear Kate,

This is a tribute to the pear tree, shimmering white last week, covered with blossoms as never before, and now all of its major limbs completely leafless. Just two upper branches in leaf. What a strange coincidence that, just a few weeks ago, when Carol stopped by to see the yard, I was telling her how excessive blossoming and fruiting is often the sign of a tree in trouble, desperately trying to reproduce before its demise, yet I didn't take notice of the pear. I should have seen it coming, what with all the downies nesting in its upper trunk, so riddled with holes there's barely anything left to carry the sap. You saw it coming a few years ago when you wanted to take it down completely, but I couldn't let it go. And I still can't. And not just because I believe in the parable of the gardener and the fruit tree. Nor just because its two remaining limbs are young and robust. Nor even because it's been standing there for more than a hundred years. No, I'm holding on because the pear has always been the apple of my eye from the day I first saw it in bloom, standing in the center of the yard, its A-shaped head like a lady in white, as stately and lovely as you.

SATURDAY, MAY 3
Dear Kate,

Yesterday morning, I was so sick to my stomach that I didn't get up until ten o'clock, but today I was able to do a few chores, like finishing the thank-you notes and seeding up the marigolds. It never occurred to me that someday I might be doing the marigolds — they were so much a part of your springtime ritual that I can still see you standing by the kitchen sink, seeding trays and trays of them for my vegetable beds and the neighborhood park. I also remember you harvesting seeds from the Disco Red marigolds just a few weeks before you died, because we couldn't find them in the catalogs. So, I'm keeping my fingers crossed, hoping they germinate. I never imagined that a germinating marigold could seem so important, but in the wake of your death all the bits and pieces of your life, all the fragments of your days and ways, are like sacred tokens that I cherish beyond all common sense. Hannah would probably tell me that I'm holding on too tight, and you would probably tell me to get on with my life. But then again, you'd probably also tell me that "it's time to start the marigolds, otherwise they won't be ready come June."

Speaking of Hannah, she sent me this e-mail yesterday — "I had a dream about Kate just before I woke up this morning. It was Thanksgiving in the dream and I had a very sweet one-year-old daughter. What I remember is that Kate was directing all the parts of putting the dinner together and instructing me in the proper way to cook cauliflower while planning to take my young baby girl off on a shopping trip. In her own inimitable way, she was the ringleader of the three-ring circus of Thanksgiving." What an enviable dream, especially compared to the anxiety dream I had last night of having to take a trip without you — you weren't well enough to travel — and I couldn't get everything packed in a single suitcase in time for the airplane's departure, until I realized, too late, that the shoulder bag you gave me a few years ago could be stuffed with everything I needed. Such different dreams that only upon reflection did I realize you were the guiding spirit in both.

MONDAY, MAY 5

Dear Kate,

Chris came over this afternoon to remove the dead limbs of the pear tree, but I decided not to watch lest I break down in the middle of his saw cuts. So much of its old trunk filled with pecker-fretted holes and nests that the amputation was bound to leave it looking like a basket case. Now that it's done, though, the tree looks much better than I imagined — not as full or expansive, but still quite shapely and robust, its leaves intensely green, its two remaining limbs covered with fruit. Such a delightful surprise that I decided to do something positive myself by starting the seeds for your flower bed in the park. But no sooner did I find your cache of old seed packets than I could feel myself choking up, and when I brought them out to the kitchen counter I was in tears, as I rummaged through the box, trying to figure out what you planted last year, until I came upon several packets held together with a big paper clip, all of them marked 2002. Finding that batch was like coming upon a treasure trove, even if most of the packets were empty. For the knowledge of what you planted was all that mattered — all I needed to replicate your flower bed this year. Do you see how desperate I am — that a mere trace of you, a notation from you to yourself, could save my day, if only because it felt like a message from you to me.

TUESDAY, MAY 6

Dear Kate,

You were back again last night in a little episode that took place in your closet — now so filled with my stuff that there's not even room for a few spare hangers. And that was the focus of the dream, for you had just returned and immediately wanted to hang up your clothes — a black silk dress and some other fancy things that I must have recalled from looking at snapshots again last night. I teased you at first for having abandoned your closet and me too — "No room at the inn," said I — but soon we were gleefully stuffing your clothes back in, as if you were come to stay, and the closet had magically expanded to fit all of our things combined, at which point I awoke, wish fulfilled.

Now all I ask is a return visit sometime before the end of next month, when the raspberries are ripe. I spent most of the day cutting out the deadwood and weeding the bed, a thorny task, especially among the blacks. But it looks like we'll have a big enough crop for fresh and jam alike. The only problem is that I don't have the slightest idea of how to make it, not even after watching you stir and stir the stuff in your copper kettle, until it was thick enough to jell, falling from your spoon just so.

WEDNESDAY, MAY 7

Dear Kate,

A picture of you that I'd never seen arrived in today's mail, with a note from Eileen, reporting that she took it some eighteen years ago, shortly after the twenty-fifth reunion of your high school class. I remember the party, remember meeting her husband, CJ, remember your telling me she was too shy to attend the reunion, remember your telling me stories of your longtime friendship with Eileen. But I don't remember you ever looking so much like Mia Farrow. Probably it's just the wave of your hair, your face tilted slightly upwards, your eyes focused on someone outside the picture who's evidently talking to you. I was also touched by Eileen's note that "she is intently listening to someone and soon will smile her beautiful smile." You were always a good listener. But I was captivated most of all by how utterly put-together you were — in your brown silk dress, handmade of course, with cloth-covered buttons over one shoulder, smartly offset by your ivory necklace, and a soft leather purse clutched under your arm. A model of good form. Looking at that shot from your early forties, I couldn't help wondering how it compared to more recent ones from your late fifties. And the surprising thing was that you still looked so young — not like Mia Farrow, but not like someone approaching sixty. You, of course, were never fooled by the illusion, always reminding me "how little time we have," but I was taken in, always imagining we could beat the odds, especially after each of us had survived a big-time illness. So I assumed we could weather the next malady and the next. How strange to be blindsided by something that neither of us imagined, not even after your father's stroke. Good doctors and a good diet, I thought, would keep us going long beyond our parents and grandparents. So much for the American dream.

FRIDAY, MAY 9

Dear Kate,

I spent this morning getting things together for your table at the Project Green plant fair. Packing up the neighborhood-tree-walk brochures was a simple matter, but deciding what else to bring was something else, given our limited space at the fair. After skimming some forty leaflets and booklets — does anyone have a bigger stockpile than you? — I decided just to bring the most basic handouts, like how to plant a tree, how to care for a tree, how to identify trees, how to choose the best trees for our area, and so on. Loading it all in the Jeep, I felt like a loyal trooper, serving the cause of Heritage Trees. But I also felt like an imposter, trying to maintain such a project without any of your know-how — a not so subtle reminder that I need to find someone who can take over. Help wanted: nonpaying director of citywide tree-preservation project; flexible hours; friendly clientele.

This afternoon I stopped over at Judy's, to give her some of my spare tomato plants and a copy of your "Chemo-Log." She's speaking at the memorial service, based on her experience as your cancer nurse, so I thought your diary might refresh her memory of things. But even without looking at your log, she remembered how optimistic you always seemed to be, and I confirmed her impressions, but also let her know how plagued you were by the side effects of tamoxifen — the early morning sweats, the peeling skin, and so on. I also told her about your refusal to join a support group because you didn't want "to become a professional breast cancer victim." I remember your saying back then, "It's bad enough I got it. I don't want to spend my life talking about it." Which makes me wonder what you'd say about these letters — now almost six months later, and I'm still writing about it. Maybe I should invoke your words and see how they work for me — "It's bad enough she's gone. I don't want to spend my life writing about it." Or do I?

SATURDAY, MAY 10
Dear Kate,

The plant fair this morning stirred up so many springtime memories of digging and planting that I decided to hold a special ceremony this afternoon, to scatter some of your ashes around the central peony in your perennial bed, your 'Festiva Maxima.' So, after a quick lunch, I carried the black vase into the kitchen, removed the dried flowers, and carefully tilted it into a plastic bag on the counter, assuming that your ashes would readily pour into the bag. But nothing came out, so I gently tapped the vase again, and again, and again, and suddenly they exploded onto the counter. Such a shocking thing that I jumped back, appalled at the sight of your ashes piled up in such an unlikely place, but then strangely delighted by the thought that you were back at the counter where you spent so much of your life the past thirty-three years. Yes, it was a dusty job getting them back in the vase and a few handfuls in the plastic bag, but the silky, gritty feel was a reminder of you. Then out to your bed I went, bag in one hand, three-pronged claw in the other, to cultivate the soil around the peony before kneeling to scatter your ashes in a complete circle. After working them in, I contemplated the bush, its buds swollen, the soil around it flecked with gray, and it felt good to know you were there at the heart of things, nurturing your favorite peony as never before. It also felt good to remember the time we made love just a few feet away on that warm summer night when my kids were here and you thought we should keep our desires to ourselves — never mind the neighbors, they were probably at it themselves. A beguiling reverie, but not enough to distract me from the rest of your bed, which I spent the afternoon weeding and hoeing to a fare-thee-well, while Puck held forth in the center of the yard, circling, circling, and the sky turned dark with a threatening storm, and the rains came, and they watered you in, watered you in.

TUESDAY, MAY 13

Dear Kate,

Trudy called this morning with the news that she'd been transferred from the side-by-side seats to Hawaii that we booked several months ago to a completely different set of flights with different departure and arrival times from mine. And she was just notified of the change, though it actually took place more than a month ago. The nightmare world of Kafka in the friendly skies of United. And it took almost two hours on the telephone with a United specialist and her supervisor to remedy the problem by transferring me to the same flights as Trudy's. Such an irritating rigmarole that I almost decided to cancel the trip and scatter the rest of your ashes in the perennial bed. For it seemed as if your invisible hand might be sending me a message — "Don't go there, don't do that!" — else why all the hassle without any knowledge of its source?

But that was nothing compared to the mistake I made this evening of watching a movie called *Wit*, about the demise of a sharp-tongued English professor, done in by ovarian cancer and an experimental reg-

imen of chemotherapy. I should have turned it off the minute it became clear that the movie would be one long, agonizing death scene.
But how could I ignore such a daredevil performance, especially by
Emma Thompson, and besides I was fascinated to see how the death
itself would be performed. Compare and contrast, hers and yours.
What I didn't expect was the morphine drip, just like yours, nor the
moment when her aged professor crawled on the hospital bed and
cradled Thompson in her arms, just as I had wanted to do with you.
Oh yes, Thompson was faintly conscious while you were miles away,
unresponsive to my words and kisses and touches. Still, I'm haunted
now by the memory of you alone on that bed and me not cradling you
in my arms.

THURSDAY, MAY 15
Dear Kate,

Hannah called first thing this morning, full of good cheer — "So
how's it going, Dad?" Too bad I couldn't answer her with equally good
humor, given a hangover from wine and kabobs and wine at David's
last night. But her buoyancy was irrepressible, so much so that I wonder if she might have been trying to cheer me up with enthusiasm for
the batch of letters that I sent her a few days ago — "I'd love to see
more whenever you're willing to send them." Sometimes, I think she's
trying to be my grief counselor and cheerleader (consciously or un-
consciously, I don't know which), and that's why she's interested in
reading the letters. But then again, why should I be uneasy about her
trying to help me? Am I too proud to be counseled by my forty-seven-
year-old daughter? Or am I too proud to be counseled by anyone? I
couldn't help pondering that question after the funeral home invited
me to join a discussion group for men who've recently lost their
wives — more of them than usual the past year. Like you, of course,
I've never been a joiner, never had a taste for group therapy, so I po-
litely refused, and thanked them for their concern. But the mere idea
of taking part was so unwelcome that it made me think I must have
been put off by something else — selfishness, shyness, cowardice,
pride, or just a deep-down inability to imagine myself talking about
something that I've been writing about every day. Enough is enough.

FRIDAY, MAY 16

Dear Kate,

Last night, I was so tired from gardening that I didn't want to give Puck his bedtime walk. But a glance out the kitchen window revealed such an enormous candle display in the park that I could hardly wait to see it up close. Linda's biggest show of all. Down to the park we ran, Puck pulling on his leash until we were a foot or two away and then he just stood there, transfixed by the light of all those candles — seventy-six, I counted them! — flickering in the grass. Such a dazzling display that others in the neighborhood were also mesmerized. I'm not sure what got into Linda, but I have a hunch she might have been inspired by my invitation to speak at your memorial. Maybe that's why she also brought me a bag of morels, the biggest ones I've ever seen. I wonder what she'll do the night before your memorial. Or after.

This evening, I went to a party in honor of Alan's retirement from the university, and it put me in mind of how foolishly distressed I was on the verge of my own. So downcast that I turned my anxiety into a journal, as if retirement were a prefiguration of death, rather than the precursor of a life we could never have had without it. How little I knew about death back then to suppose that anything might be the prefigurement of it, but the thing itself, which is always in the wings, but never on stage until its entrance is immutable. A thought which turned me into a desperate counselor this evening, when Ruedi told me he was scheduled to give a lecture in England this September, and Cecile said she was reluctant to go, since there'd be little in bloom at the great English estates. Before your passing, I too might have thought that way, but this evening I found myself pleading with Cecile to join him, while Ruedi stood by nodding in agreement with my cautionary tale. Gradually, she too nodded in agreement, which made me feel as if I might have made a real difference in their lives, until, of course, I realized that nothing makes such a difference but death itself.

SATURDAY, MAY 17

Dear Kate,

Trudy called to confirm that she's coming on Tuesday and will stay for a week or so, helping me get ready for the service and the buffet. Maybe we'll also visit the Rochester cemetery, in memory of the times you took me there on my birthday. You always said, "It's a perfect time to see the wildflowers in bloom," but I always wondered if you also thought it was a perfect time to put me in mind of my mortality. Now I can hardly forget it, given that my birthday comes just a day before your memorial service. Talk about strange coincidences! Too bad I couldn't have scheduled it earlier, but then the trees wouldn't have been in leaf, and out-of-towners wouldn't have had a long weekend for travel.

Just to be sure that everything is in order at the grove, I spent a couple of hours there this morning with Karin, who's still so devoted to the project that she's promised to maintain the recently planted trees until they're all well established. Today we made an inventory of the ones that didn't leaf out — most of them white oaks. A simple enough matter, you might suppose, except that we had trouble matching up the trees in question with the ones on your diagram of the grove. After a few false starts, Karin said, "It sure is different here without her," and I could hardly disagree. After the inventory, we weeded around the fenced-in trees, so they'll look good for the memorial service. A menial enough task that we could do it without your guidance. But by the time we left, the air was heavy and I was feeling washed out, so I spent the rest of the day with the Sunday *Times*. The only problem is that I snacked all afternoon and ate too much at dinner. Sometimes, I'm so hungry for want of you that it feels like I'm starving to death, and no amount of food will help.

SUNDAY, MAY 18

Dear Kate,

I've been spending so much time on your memorial service that I'm sure you think I'm going overboard, way overboard, as if I were trying to prove something, say, like I loved you more than you ever imagined. So much so that I'm making you a Taj Mahal of a memorial service, whereas your expectations were so modest that all you said in your funeral directive was, "If someone wishes to plan a memorial service, I'd like it to be held outside in a place like the Nancy Seiberling grove." Spare and self-deprecating as ever. But the truth is that I simply want it to be a fitting tribute to you and everything you did in your life. Something that will enable others to hear your story, set it down in the tablets of their memory, and say to themselves, as I sometimes have at other such affairs, "I didn't know she did all those things." Taking stock as we all do whenever we take stock of a life. That's why it's taking place in the grove you designed and planted, that's why thirteen people are speaking in memory of you, each one bearing witness to a different aspect of your life, that's why the memorial booklet contains so many pictures of you at different times in your life. As full an accounting as possible, that memory may be served. Yet I also know that no matter how well it turns out, the service and the booklet and the flutist and the buffet will not only celebrate your life but also mark a formal closure of it, from which the community moves on, while I can't possibly do so. Which makes me wonder why I'm devoting so much time to such a transient thing, a one-time happening, a blowout, that will probably leave me feeling even more bereft than before, especially without such a consuming project to distract me. And all I can think of right now is to tell you that the excess of it all is a but a tiny emblem of what you gave to me and others in the course of your life. So, after all, the more lavish it is the more true it will be to you. And the transience of it? That too is in keeping with your life.

MONDAY, MAY 19

Dear Kate,

Raeburn and I met downtown this morning, to review the program for the service and the exact order of the speakers. I hadn't realized that he's such a stickler for details, though I should have known, given how meticulous he was as chair of the department. Today, for example, just when I thought that everything was done, he urged me to send all the speakers a list indicating the order of their appearance, together with a letter suggesting that they introduce themselves, not only for the audience, but also as a cue for each of them to follow.

And I thought it would be a classically simple affair. Simple, as I've discovered, is by definition complex. For example, in the course of writing the speakers this afternoon, I got a call from the funeral home, reporting that the rental agency for the tent (in case of rain) requires that we pay for it — four-hundred dollars — whether we use the tent or not. Would I rather use the wooden pavilion (free of charge)? No, I'd rather have the tent and be amid the trees, which I assume is what you would have wanted. Which raised another question — would I like to have the tent set up on Saturday, so that we use it and get our money's worth, rain or shine? No, I'd rather not set it up until some-time Sunday morning, and only if it's definitely needed, since the pur-pose of holding the service in the grove is to see and feel the pres-ence of the trees above us and all around us, even if it means spending four-hundred dollars on a tent we never use. Once the tent question was resolved, I suddenly found myself fretting about whether the fu-neral home will put up signs pointing toward the service, and whether there'll be people to guide traffic, and whether I should order a special bouquet of flowers. A bouquet for the service! — why didn't I think of that until now? I wonder what else I'll remember tomorrow.

TUESDAY, MAY 20

Dear Kate,

Trudy arrived late this afternoon, so I spent much of the day clean-ing and shopping. But the most important business took place first thing this morning at the florist's, where I ordered a special bouquet, white on white — the largest they make — so it'll stand out in the green, green setting of the grove. Lilies, peonies, tulips, dendrobium orchids (in celebration of your love for Hawaii), and a few sprigs of larkspur for contrast. I also bought enough flowers to put together some bouquets for Trudy, but those were nothing compared to the one I put together on a whim, as if guided by you. It all started with some leftover greens that I used as backing for a few of the large pink tulips you planted last fall. Then I noticed three rust brown tulips by the terrace wall and picked them too. And they made all the difference. Such a striking combination of colors and shapes that it looked like the work of your hand. Trudy thought so too, when she arrived a while later. And she looked like a bouquet as well, her gray hair so striking, her color so radiant that it was hard to believe she'd been short of breath in Wyoming. And I told her so. But then I remembered how ra-diant you looked the night before you died and kept that thought to myself. Trudy, in turn, told me how wonderful I look, which led me to imagine that grief might be the making of me, though it's probably just the result of gardening without my sunhat. Whatever the cause, I can't help thinking that the supposed correlation between good looks and well-being is a grand illusion, perpetrated by the tyranny of our eyes. Only the blind are undeceived.

THURSDAY, MAY 22

Dear Kate,

Sometimes it feels as if everything I do these days is a reminder of you. As if I'm trapped in the rhythm of a memorial service, everything echoing your words and deeds. Today it was the tomato plants, so leggy and overgrown that I'm sure you'd have thought they should already be in the ground. What else to do, then, but plant the tomatoes? Yet how strange it felt to perform that springtime ritual with Trudy rather than you. Stranger still to ponder the number of plants I need — a handful at most, maybe no more than two or three — when just a year ago we lengthened the bed to make room for fifteen. But something within me resisted such a drastic reduction. All your canning jars in the basement waiting to be refilled. And your juicer to be turned again, and your dryer put to use. So I settled on nine, enough to provide bounty for friends and neighbors as well as for me. Planting and staking them was a breeze but fencing them with last year's tangle of bamboo poles and deer mesh was hardly a pleasure, even with the help of Trudy. No sooner did we start untangling the mesh than I remembered the afternoon that you helped me bundle it up just a week before you died. You were so impatient to be done and back to your reading that I was sorry to have bothered you. But the memory of my guilt was nothing compared to the memory of you, oak basket in hand, opening the mesh gate, entering the tomato patch, harvesting the fruit, hovering over your canning pots, summer in and summer out, all the summers of our lives.

FRIDAY, MAY 23

Dear Kate,

First thing this morning, I went to the co-op for a case of wine, a case of Pellegrino, several pounds of asparagus, a half-dozen lemons, fifteen pounds of pork tenderloin, and a cup of coffee to keep me humming. Stocking up for the postservice buffet. Then back home to pick up the living room, pick up the dining room, straighten up the kitchen, then dust, then vacuum, then eyeball the house beautiful. Ready for all the out-of-town guests. Then off to the airport for Martha and Rachel. A simple enough matter until I first saw Rachel in the middle distance — not just your niece, but such a knockoff of you in the backward abysm of time that I could hardly believe it. No, not a replica — her face is round rather than long, her complexion ruddy rather than pale, her hair dark brown rather than reddish brown. But there were resemblances enough in her eyebrows, her eyes, her bearing, her height, and her jaunty clothes to remind me of you when we first met. So of course I relished her warm embrace, but then felt like an old man warped by grief and time. Thank God for Martha's twangy hello, and Trudy to introduce, and dinner to cook. And no sooner did we get home than Hannah and Amy arrived, then Marshall and Kathleen, with so many hugs and so much talk that I almost forgot myself and you in the din of welcomes and dinner and a visit to the grove. But you were there and not there, in the foreground and the background all evening long — a haunting presence, especially at bedtime, when the others had gone to their motel, and I was here with just Martha and Rachel, versions of all that I long for.

SATURDAY, MAY 24

Dear Kate,

Shortly after breakfast, Hannah and Amy arrived with two freshly baked apple pies from Kalona and a "Happy Birthday, Dad!" How touching, I thought, given the pie you always baked for my birthday. But how strange, I felt, to be celebrating my birthday during your memorial days. Kathleen touched me too with an eloquent birthday poem about the grove, celebrating you and our love for each other. Some granddaughter! And Martha put me in my place with a Tampa Bay Buccaneers t-shirt — I bet against them in the Super Bowl and paid her with a case of beer when I was down in Florida. Her smart-ass gift reminded me of the Bush family cutout-book that you ordered a week before you died and that I forgot to send her for Christmas. So we had an amusing exchange before the day turned serious with preparations for tomorrow. Martha, the fanatic housecleaner, took on the kitchen, living room, and dining room, all of which I vacuumed and dusted on Tuesday and again yesterday, but none of which were up to her standards. Marshall attacked the driveway, back porch, and terrace, turning the accumulated mess of this spring into a scene from *House and Garden*. And I prepared the food for tomorrow — roast pork tenderloins, steamed and chilled asparagus, lemon mayonnaise, tomato aspic — feeling all the while as if I were marching to the beat of your drum. Some birthday. But virtue was rewarded when Hannah, Marshall, and Amy took me to dinner at the Mekong, along with Kathleen, Martha, Rachel, Peter, and Trudy. Such a buoyant occasion, all of us spread around a circular banquet table, that it almost felt like a family reunion of sorts, a festive homecoming, as if nothing were missing or amiss.

SUNDAY, MAY 25

Dear Kate,

I woke at five and couldn't get back to sleep — all keyed up for the day. What else to do but get things ready for the buffet. Platters, plates, placemats, glasses, silverware, napkins, the whole shebang. Setups in the dining room, seating on the terrace, plants in the gazebo. Everything fussed to death, until the next wave of family arrived — your cousins, your in-laws, most of them together for the first time since Lib died and you orchestrated a gathering like this, just before we headed off for China. Once again the handshakes and the hugs. Again the group portrait by the terrace wall. Faces creased again with the bittersweet smiles of sorrow and reunion. Everyone in their Sunday best, as crisp and vivid as the day itself. A day so clear and mild, so different from the rainy forecast, that it must have been blessed by the gods or by you. No tent, thank you! Nothing to distract from the grove itself, shimmering in the tree-filtered light — the grass freshly mown, though it had already been mowed at the beginning of the week. A surprising tribute from the city's Park Department. And the white wooden chairs? Another surprise — I could hardly believe how pristine they looked amid all that green, like an idyllic setting for a chautauqua, and a perfect match for the white bouquet.

The service itself was as simple and stately as the setting — from the elegant flutist to the eloquent tributes to the enduring plea of the Lord's Prayer and "America the Beautiful." The only problem is that I found myself strangely impassive through the whole thing, and I don't know why, for I thought it would unstring me. Maybe I was too conscious of myself and of others sitting nearby. Or too aware of my carefully organized program — an anxious producer rather than a mournful husband — hanging on every word and gesture, hoping that everything would go off without a hitch, that every speaker would have a memorable story, a vivid image, a striking turn of phrase. Or perhaps I was just too exhausted from weeks of planning and nights of fretting. So tired of it all that a couple of times this week I could hardly wait for it to be over and done with. And it wasn't much better during the buffet. So many things to be done, like slicing the pork, slicing the bread, unmolding the aspic, opening and pouring the wine, arranging everything attractively on the tables, that I can see why you felt so exhausted after the one you did for Lib. Still, it was a pleasure to behold the terrace full of friends and relatives, breaking bread, sipping wine. All except for Hannah, alone in a lawn chair looking out toward the backyard, overcome with a sense of your absence. Also touching to hear cousin David urge that "sometime we should get together just for the fun of it rather than the grief of it." And then the day-trippers gradually drifting away, until it was just the eight of us again, at the neighborhood park in the cool of the evening, to observe Linda's candles and add a few of our own.

MONDAY, MAY 26
Dear Kate,

Amy and Hannah took off after breakfast, Peter a while later, Martha and Rachel after lunch, so it felt more like moving day than Memorial Day, even when the mournful sound of taps came wafting over from the cemetery in midmorning. A time to pause and reflect, but I was in the garden with Kathleen, watering the vegetables — we haven't had rain for three weeks — and she was telling me about her plan to prepare for doctoral study by majoring in anthropology and minoring in philosophy and political science. An incoming freshman at Smith and already thinking about graduate school! As intense and serious as you must have been heading off to Vassar, full of your desire to be a poet-playwright in the grand Shakespearean manner. Listening to Kathleen envision her career, I couldn't help wondering how she'll deal with the ambushes of life, the disappointments to come. They always do for someone with her ambitions — or yours. My thoughts just then were deeply tinged by a consciousness of your story, and the way you often referred to it as "a wasted life." As if the fate of your plays were the measure of your life. How different from the speakers who remembered you yesterday afternoon, bearing witness to so many different facets of your life that people came away shaking their heads in amazement. "I had no idea she did so many wonderful things" is what I heard one woman saying to another. Hearing such words, I felt a rare sense of satisfaction that your light was no longer hidden under a bushel, but also a keen sense of regret that you weren't there for the unveiling. And an overwhelming sense of the absurd that your life might never have been perceived that way had each speaker not talked about a distinctly different aspect of it. The truth of one's existence is often so complex that no one can ever see it whole, especially not the person in question. Maybe that's the purpose of a memorial service — not just to celebrate a life, but to illuminate it with the light of other lives.

FRIDAY, JUNE 6

Dear Kate,

Talk about a hangover — that's how I've been feeling ever since the memorial weekend. Ten days like a half-dead zombie, unable to get myself in gear enough even to write you a brief letter. Oh yes, I paid the bills, weeded your perennial bed, chatted with Lara about her new book project, and so on. But that hardly adds up to ten days' worth of anything. I've been so tired, achy, and constipated that I thought my thyroid was failing again, until Karl told me two days ago that the hormone level is normal. Which means that something else is causing the trouble, as I should have known even before Hannah called to report that she and Amy were so exhausted from the weekend they could hardly drag themselves to work or think about anything else. "Join the club, Dad," is the way that Hannah put it when I told her about my troubles, but I didn't believe it could affect me that way until I checked the medical encyclopedia last night and discovered that constipation can also be caused by extreme depression and/or exhaustion. So I've been taking Metamucil the last few days, and things started taking their course a couple of sentences ago. Already my mood is improving.

But not enough to overcome the vacuum I've been feeling in the wake of the memorial service. I should have foreseen it coming, should have been aware that I'd feel so empty-handed when it was all over that I wouldn't have anything to tell you about except feeling empty-handed, especially without a project or deadline to keep me going from here on out. Last week, I was buoyed up by a wave of phone calls, e-mails, and cards about the service and you. But that only lasted a few days, and even while it was going on I could see it was a fleeting thing, like reading reviews of one's latest work. So I tried to fill the space with editorial chores for Holly, but now that I've finished the manuscripts there's nothing to do for the press. And pleasing as it is to work in the garden, tending your perennials and my vegetables, the spectacle soon palls, especially without you here to see for yourself how much more lush and beautiful things are this spring.

In other words, I've been suffering such a case of the blahs, of life without an ostensible purpose, that I haven't been up to a daily letter. And the more I've put off writing, the guiltier I've become, especially when I remember your perennial admonition that "guilt is not a useful feeling. Just pull up your socks and do something about it." And so I have, at least for the moment.

SATURDAY, JUNE 7

Dear Kate,

Last night, when I called my brother to wish him a happy birthday — his seventy-sixth — he told me that he delivered three lectures last week. Almost as good, he said, as before his stroke. A remarkable comeback from death's door just a year ago. He also assured me that he's taking extra naps to compensate for the stress and that he won't be doing any professional work during the next few weeks in Sardinia. Just sun and sea and sand. I could tell that he was trying to allay my anxiety about the perils of such a long-distance flight. But he needn't have bothered, for I found myself strangely untroubled by his doings — delighted even that he could get on his horse and ride it again, right into the sunset. In part, I suppose, it's a belated acceptance of the way things are with him and Phyllis. They love to travel, and I can hardly blame them for continuing to do it while they're both alive, especially when I think of the trips that we had planned before you died.

And judging from my week in Florida, the thought of traveling without you doesn't make me yearn for distant shores. This evening, though, I got all the way to Newfoundland, thanks to a DVD of *The Shipping News*, about a man who loses his wife, but finds a new life in a country far from home, which turns out to be the home of his ancestors. How's that for a pipe dream?

MONDAY, JUNE 9

Dear Kate,

Last week, when I was too zonked to write, I got a call from Carol, prefaced with an apology, asking me when I might be ready to be fixed up. "Fixed up" — I haven't heard the expression in years, and never realized until now what a double-edged phrase it is. As if a blind date could repair me. Carol was not doing the fixing, but was calling on behalf of a friend, who had asked her to be in touch. Matchmaker, matchmaker! Well, you can imagine what I said — or perhaps you can't. "Please tell her I'm grateful for the thought, but the answer is 'not now, not ever.'" I went on a bit with Carol to explain myself, telling her that I didn't think it would be fair to you, and certainly wouldn't be tolerable for any woman I might get involved with, given my irrepressible thoughts of you. She completely understood, of course, but afterward I couldn't help thinking of how you and I had both wished that your mother might take up with someone in the years after your father's death. In fact, I remember how appalled you were by the ferocity of her anger when she came back from the funeral, took off her hat, shoved a long hairpin through it, and said, "That's that, I'll never let it happen to me again." So I couldn't help wondering if my response to Carol was akin to your mother's — closing myself off in a way that would leave me as emotionally bereft and barren as she. Which brings me to a conversation that I had with Trudy, who's back in New Jersey and called this afternoon to catch up on things since the memorial. I told her about the call from Carol, told her about my suddenly mixed feelings, and her response was surprisingly firm: "You had something with Kate that was very special, that most people only dream of having, and you had it for most of your adult life. Which makes me think you should consider yourself lucky, very lucky, especially when I think of the marriage I had and how risky it is to get involved with someone, and so many ways to go wrong." Though tinged with disappointment, her advice made sense, except for a remarkable air of hopefulness when she went on to assure me that "something will come into your life, you'll find something sooner or later, and you'll know it right off when the time comes." But right now I don't know what it might be, if it isn't in the garden, isn't in my head, or isn't in any of the movies I've been seeing. Mostly right now, I feel like a mourning dove without its mate, especially compared to the twosome that just turned up at the feeder. Maybe I should take down the feeder, as you always urged me to do in April — then I won't have to see them together and they won't get hooked on summer handouts.

WEDNESDAY, JUNE 11

Dear Kate,

This evening, I watched a DVD of *American Beauty* — such a scathing vision of contemporary culture and family life that I found it compelling from start to finish. Except at the very end, when the deceased narrator, looking back on the moment of his death, remembers how he was enchanted just then by so many beautiful images from his life. How could that have been possible, I wondered, given that he must have died instantly when his brains were blown out by a shot from behind the head that he was completely unaware of until the bullet was fired? Implausible, to say the least. And worse still, a travesty of the cliché that our lives sweep before us in our dying moments. I wonder what you were seeing or thinking in your final moments, when you were so carried away by morphine that it seems inconceivable you were seeing or thinking of anything. Ever since you died, I've been thinking so much about dying that I can hardly see it in the movies or read about it in fiction without a reflexively skeptical or critical view of the depiction. As if anyone could ever know such an unknowable thing.

MONDAY, JUNE 16

Dear Kate,

Today, for the first time ever, I made myself a cherry cobbler with fruit from our tree. The only problem is that it wasn't made according to Hoyle or according to you. I didn't pit enough cherries for a full recipe, so I had to reduce all the flavoring and thickening measurements by one quarter of the specified amounts. I didn't have enough butter on hand when I started making the dough, so I had to make an emergency run to the store in midcourse. I added too much milk to the flour, which made the dough so sticky that I couldn't knead it, much less get it off my fingers and palms without scraping it away with a knife. Then in desperation I added so much flour to the sticky wad to make it kneadable that I screwed up the ratio of flour to baking powder, but didn't realize my mistake until the cobbler was already in the oven. I also used too large a pie plate for the quantity of fruit, but didn't realize my error until I pulled the cobbler from the oven and watched the bubbling mass settle down into a disarmingly thin layer of fruit. Worse still, my circles of dough, attractively arranged though they were and nicely browned, didn't remind me of yours at all — not light and fluffy enough by far. Next time I'll know better and prepare my dough more carefully from start to finish. Next time I'll also have some vanilla ice cream on hand to go with the oven-warm cobbler, just as you and your mother always did. Next time, I'll invite someone for dessert, for there's nothing quite so forlorn as a solitary cobbler.

SUNDAY, JUNE 22

Dear Kate,

When I got up this morning, all I could think of was the prospect of going to the neighborhood picnic without you. All week long, in fact, I've been hoping it might be rained out, especially since we've gone two weeks without a drop. But the day dawned sunny, so I had to go through all your rigmarole alone — not only making a dish for the potluck, but also taking care of the other things you always provided, like the tablecloths, the paper plates and cups, the condiments and so on, not to mention my own job of helping to get the shelter and tables ready. But it wasn't the work so much as the memory of you last year at this time, all got up in your bright summer jumper, picking flowers from your perennial bed to make bouquets for each of the picnic tables. The memory of you and those bouquets — that's what almost did me in. But thanks to the camaraderie of neighbors, helping me set up the shelter and the tables, I got through the morning in good order, and then, believe it or not, someone showed up with hand-picked flowers for each of the picnic tables and pictures from last fall's picnic, and the food was good and the talk so lively that I almost got through it without regret.

TUESDAY, JUNE 24

Dear Kate,

It was so hot today — 96 with a heat index of 110! — that I turned on the air conditioner for the first time this summer and ran it non-stop. Probably I should have started it yesterday, given the warmup that began on Sunday and the accumulated heat of the brick walls radiating inside all night long. The house was so uncomfortable for a while that it reminded me of that blistering summer day in the mid 1970s when I came home and found you slightly crazed from the heat — your otherwise impeccable judgment so affected that you thought we could solve the problems of this three-story place with a window air conditioner rather than a central cooling system. But no sooner did I get the house cooled off than I remembered the downside of being confined in an artificial air system. The cooled air is too cool, the hot air outside is even hotter by contrast, and the constant hum of the motor sounds like the incessant noise of a long airplane flight. No wonder you were reluctant to use it except in a heat wave and even then refused to run it all night long. But I also remember all those wacky nights when no sooner did you ask me to turn it off and open the windows than you told me to shut the windows and turn it on again — chiding me for the intolerable heat even though I warned you in advance. What else but the heat and the different thermometers inside us could provoke such loony tensions — and affections? I was thinking of that — of how opposites collide with each other and enflame each other — when I was watching *Possession* this evening. Not a very good movie, after all — a watered-down version of Byatt's labyrinthine novel — but even the bare-boned difference of the two literary scholars (she always so put together, he often so reckless) was enough to remind me of what brought us together and kept us together all these years. Such different fires burning within us — how could we fail to keep each other warm?

WEDNESDAY, JUNE 25

Dear Kate,

Thanks to a cold front and a rip-roaring thunderstorm, I turned off the air conditioning this afternoon. But the heat all morning and the rain all afternoon kept me inside all day, so I decided to make the most of it by starting on a chore I've been putting off ever since your memorial service. As in, sending copies of the memorial booklet to family and friends who were unable to attend the service. A simple matter, you might think, but I didn't feel it would be right just to send people the keepsake without a brief note of explanation or a response to their condolences of last fall, so I've been reading the cards and letters again, making myself more anguished than I've felt in a long while, as if my grief were green again, called into being anew by all those words of solace. How strange, that words of comfort should cause such pain — that even now, seven months later, I'm still so vulnerable. At this point, I suppose, you might tell me, "Don't go there, stop dwelling on it, do something constructive, otherwise you'll wind up like my mother, a professional griever." But what would you say if I told you there's a box of two hundred booklets left over from the service? Trash them? More likely, you'd tell me, "Don't waste them, not after you've gone to the trouble and expense of having them printed." So, I've got a new project of sorts to keep me busy, and when this is done I can put all the condolences away or include them with your papers for the library. Or whatever it takes to be done with the grieving.

FRIDAY, JUNE 27

Dear Kate,

Shortly after lunch, Carol called with the news that John died last night — free at last from the afflictions of a brain tumor and advanced age as well as the numbing side effects of radiation therapy. He was hardly able to hear or see or speak the last time I saw him several months ago — a far cry from when you, I, and Carol celebrated his ninety-fourth birthday with a special lunch, and he was working his way through a videotaped course in astronomy. Who could possibly have imagined that a year later you'd be gone, and he'd be so diminished? And who could sensibly want to continue living with such diminished capacities? Yet when Carol called, my immediate reaction — "How sad" or words to that effect — was so inappropriate, so knee-jerky, that I'm embarrassed to report it. Oh yes, I quickly corrected myself and told her, "He's best out of it." And she agreed. But now I'm troubled by that cliché, as well as another one I uttered several weeks ago, when I told Holly that he's a cautionary example for anyone desiring such a long life. Given such a limited and impoverished set of responses, I'm inclined just to shut up and say nothing, except, "What can I say?" Which is also a cliché. Better, perhaps, just to think of what a splendid person he was — how generous, self-deprecating, and witty. Also how ambitious, in the best sense of that word, for the department, the university, and the profession. Come to think of it, had he not hired me forty years ago, I don't know what would have come of me professionally — or personally, for without being here in Iowa, I surely would not have met you. So in a very real sense, I owe him the best years of my life. Another cliché, but true to my experience, so I'll leave it as is. I owe him the best years of my life.

SUNDAY, JUNE 29
Dear Kate,

The news of this day is that Katharine Hepburn died at the age of ninety-six. The television stations, of course, ran pictures of her, all the way back to the earliest movies. Shots that put me in mind of what my colleagues and friends often said after they first met you — "She looks like the younger Katharine Hepburn." Well, in truth, you did and you didn't. But I think what led them to make the connection was not just your looks but your way of saying what you thought, very much like her, without ever mincing any words. I was thinking of your way with words all afternoon, thanks to a letter from Laura, in which she put it so well, so accurately, that I want you to hear it word for word: "When I think of her I think of the challenge she made me feel to be honest about my feelings and beliefs. What she said cut the air like a knife and I don't mean that she injured feelings at all, only that she was always so clear and clean in the way she spoke. She said what she meant to say and I admired her for it tremendously." Sometimes, that's what I miss most of all — your voice, your words, cutting the air like a knife.

MONDAY, JUNE 30

Dear Kate,

Carol had me over for dinner last night, together with her daughter Myriam, and Myriam's partner, Jim, both of them public service lawyers for prisoners on death row. It was the first time I'd seen Myriam in several years, and I was touched not only by her lawyerly poise and idealism, but also by her evident respect and affection for Jim. Which moved me, in a thoughtless moment, to tell her, "Don't wait too long." To which she swiftly replied, "Don't wait too long for what? To have babies?" There was a scornful edge in her voice, and rightly so, given my sloppily vague admonition, which sounded, I suddenly realized, like a chauvinist's urge to procreate. But that wasn't what I had in mind at all, as I quickly explained — I was only concerned about the brevity of life, and thus the urgency of their being together more often, living together rather than apart. I was thinking, of course, about how much of our lives we spent together, only apart a few days each year, and then only in the early years of our marriage, when I was doing consulting. I can hardly imagine any other way to be in love, though perhaps if we had lived in separate cities like Myriam and Jim — she in New Orleans, he in Houston — I'd be more readily adjusted to your absence. Maybe the way to deal with loss, or even prevent it, is never to be together too long. Maybe absence makes the heart beat calmer.

THURSDAY, JULY 3

Dear Kate,

The good news is that the tomatoes are setting, the zucchini are swelling, and our real-estate stock is rising. The bad news is that the temperature is soaring and our air conditioner broke down last night. And thereby hangs a tale.

I got a repairman here this morning, and an hour later, just when he thought it was fixed, the motor short-circuited — shutting down the blower each time he started it up. Nothing to do but repair it or replace it — a simple enough problem, until the manager called two hours later to report that the motor has been discontinued and is not available anywhere in the country. So much for our top-of-the-line system. The upshot is that our upstairs unit will have to be completely replaced at a cost of twenty-five hundred dollars — twenty-eight hundred if I want it installed on Saturday. Given the continuing heat wave (and our rising stock), I decided to splurge. And patted myself on the back for taking it so calmly. But I couldn't help thinking of that insufferable July evening the summer of 1995, when the temperature hit 105, and the air conditioner broke down while you were making peach jam, and the plumber fixed it that evening with the replacement of a little capacitor for the cost of forty dollars. Small change compared to this go-around, and I don't even have any jam to console me.

FRIDAY, JULY 4

Dear Kate,

No fireworks here today, but there's been so much snap, crackle, and pop in the neighborhood that it sounded like any other Fourth. But I decided to forego the usual festivities, since I didn't relish the prospect of smiling friends and colleagues looking sadly my way, as they did at David's a few weeks ago. I'm learning, learning the things that cause me pain, and learning to avoid them. "Needless pain," as you were wont to say, "is needless." Besides, it was pleasant enough just hanging out alone, catching the cool breezes of early morning and holding them in with shutters all afternoon. By evening, though, it was so heated up I could hardly bear it inside, even with my shirt off. No choice but to sit on the terrace, the bare skin of my back against the cool metal of your grandmother's lawn chairs. The only problem was that sitting in those chairs with Puck in my lap took me back to our earliest summers here, before the air-conditioning, when you'd sit on the terrace with Crispin in your lap, watching the fireflies, waiting for breezes to come our way. The breezes never came last night but the tears did and a soliloquy so full of self-pity that it was embarrassing to think the neighbors might have overheard me. Better to watch a movie, I thought, and *Shower* seemed like just the right thing, given its opening comic portrait of a new-age Chinese businessman, cellphone and all, visiting his taciturn father who owns an old-style neighborhood bathhouse. But midway through the movie, the father suddenly dies and the businessman is faced with the challenge not only of tending the bathhouse but also of caring for his lively but retarded brother. In other words, I found myself watching a movie about death, grief, and reconciliation — deeply touched by the suddenness of the brothers' loss, but intensely put off by the speed of their adjustment. Movie time, of course, is a fraction of real time, but grief, I'm sure, can hardly be assuaged so quickly, even in a deeply repressed culture.

SUNDAY, JULY 6
Dear Kate,

Hannah made her weekly checkup call this afternoon, but this time it took an unusual turn, somewhat like an echo of Carol's matchmaking call last month. It all started when she asked me the usual question, and I gave her a somewhat different answer — not talking so much about my grief and anguish as about my solitude and loneliness. Which led her to wonder whether I might be interested in the possibility of another relationship. But I rejected it so bluntly and abruptly that Hannah pursued it even more doggedly. "You never can tell what might happen, Dad." Nothing, I argued, could possibly happen without my willingness for something to happen, which provoked her to ask the ultimate question, "And why aren't you willing? Do you really want to spend the rest of your life without any such attachment?" I couldn't help wondering just then if she was thinking about something between me and Trudy, for it seemed as if Hannah and Amy had taken a liking to her during the memorial weekend. Also as if they were watching us that weekend, especially after I told them about Trudy coming to Hanalei in November. But I didn't want to ask if that's what she had in mind. For I thought it more important to ask her this — "And how would you feel if you knew that my being involved with another woman would inescapably complicate the state of your feelings about Kate? And beyond that, how would you feel about my bringing another woman and her family and all her emotional baggage into your life?" No sooner had I asked those questions than she backed off, acknowledging that "I see what you mean. I never thought about that."

TUESDAY, JULY 8
Dear Kate,

Day seven of the air-conditioning saga and day seven of the heat wave — in other words, another insufferable day. Yesterday, I didn't even bother to write, given the preposterous turn of events that started when Dan — we're now on a first-name basis — checked and re-checked the outside unit, gave it a clean bill of health, and concluded that the only remaining culprit must be the outside fuse box. Which led to my calling an electrician, who replaced the fuse box and strode off with the assurance that "it's all taken care of." And believe it or not, I believed him, until twenty minutes later when the outside unit stopped running again, and he returned again with the cocksure declaration that "it must be a faulty circuit breaker," and when that didn't solve the problem announced that it must be the outside unit: "If it was my house I'd replace that thing, a new one'll pay for itself." So, after break-fast I put in a call to Jack, manager of the plumbing firm, to order a new unit. And no sooner did I tell him what I wanted than he said, "That's exactly what I was going to suggest after what happened yesterday af-ternoon. The only way to fix it for sure is to put in a new one." No, I don't have any more illusions. In fact, I almost burst out laughing when he talked about fixing it "for sure."

Now I'm beginning to appreciate your automatic distrust of such definitive statements. Now, too, I'm beginning to understand why you sometimes lost patience with my perennial confidence in things, even when they started to turn sour. Maybe it was because I survived the slings and arrows of an orphan's life that I instinctively felt we could deal with anything that came our way — cancer, heart disease, or a broken-down air conditioner. I was thinking about that this after-noon when I got a packet of old snapshots in the mail from my cousin George — pictures not only of my mother, father, and other ancestors but also of my brother and me. What a sad-sack kid I was, my head down in every shot, as if I was embarrassed to show my face, embar-rassed even to exist, whereas your childhood pictures always show you with your head up, eyes bright, and a big smile from ear to ear. No wonder you spoke of growing up in a world "like Mother Goose." But then again, no wonder everything thereafter must have seemed like a terrible falling-off or a reason for being profoundly skeptical of things. At this point, I can imagine you saying, "It's a big stretch from child-hood snapshots to human destiny, or from air conditioning to philos-ophy." But that's where I am these days, "between two worlds, one dead, the other powerless to be born."

FRIDAY, JULY 11

Dear Kate,

No more Mister Nice Guy! That's the message for today, and I delivered it calmly but emphatically to Jack, after another surprising twist in the air-conditioning saga, when Dan finished installing the new outside unit, and it short-circuited ten minutes after he started it up, with no plausible explanation, until he called in a cohort, who promptly went up to the attic, checked on the inside unit, and discovered that it was freezing up from insufficient outlets for its cold air. In other words, it appears that we didn't need a new outside unit, didn't need a new outside fuse box, and God knows what else we didn't need. I won't bore you with the details of our conversation, except to report that I was as stern and chilly as you were when the family business was being mismanaged after your father's death. And there were apologies, as well as adjustments, and promises to have the new outlets installed first thing Monday morning. So much sweet talk, I was dripping with it, but all I could think of just then was your cautionary mantra, "Seeing is believing, especially with contractors." Speaking of which, Steve showed up an hour or so after Jack, with a new screen for the big attic window, and we had a good laugh about the air-conditioning saga. But you should have seen the look on his face when he discovered that the screen was too large for the window. The mismeasurement, he told me, was the fault of the lumberyard, and I didn't doubt him, given Steve's precision in all things. Still, I couldn't help wondering why he didn't measure it himself. But I kept my mouth shut and we had another good laugh about my bad luck. I just hope it changes by Monday.

MONDAY, JULY 14

Dear Kate,

Now that the heat wave is past, the air conditioner is finally working, thanks to Dan's installation of additional air outlets. Just two hours of work that could have solved the problem some ten days ago, which makes me wonder what caused all the mistaken remedies, all the trial and error and error. Dan's inexperience with our SpacePak air conditioner, or Jack's lack of oversight, or the electrician's bravado, or all of the above? Or none of the above? It's not that I'm interested in laying the blame on someone — it might even be me for lack of having an annual check before the problem occurred. No, I'm interested in the sources of human error and why remedies go wrong, as they might have done in your case. I'm thinking, for example, of the aspirin you took each day in the wake of your ischemic attack several years ago — a twenty-second episode that put you on aspirin that might have exacerbated or even caused the hemorrhage. I'm also thinking of how you and your doctors were so focused on preventing the return of your cancer that everyone overlooked your high blood pressure, which might also have led to the hemorrhage. Whenever I talk this way with Amy, she always tells me that it doesn't do any good. But then again, what good does it do if error persists without remorse or remedy? I wonder, for example, if I'm doing the right thing by continuing to write you these letters some eight months after your demise — keeping in touch but also keeping my grief alive in ways that silence might assuage.

MONDAY, JULY 21

Dear Kate,

Things are changing around here, changing in ways you'd probably oppose, but they're changing just the same. It all started with an overnight downpour and a wind so strong that the rain must have blown through the stairway window, arced over the bannister and landed on the radiator cover below, where Rowley's shots of you were propped against the stairway — the art board so wrinkled that the only thing to do was get them matted and framed, as I should have in the first place. And that was just the beginning of things. For no sooner did I decide to have them framed than I remembered some other things to be done at the framer's. The watercolor of the oak leaves that slipped loose from its backing a few months ago. The Chinese hanging of a mountainside landscape that you bought in Chongqing but never decided what to do with — frame it or hang the scroll just as is. So an ill wind blew me down to the framer's, where they assured me there'd be no problem remounting the watercolor. They also suggested that I hang the Chinese scroll just as is, and see how it looks before deciding whether or not to frame it. Then I went through the maze of picking out a mat and frame for the shots of you, two of which I'll hang in the study, so you'll always be visible when I go there to write. The third one

I'll prop against the stairway in the living room, so you're visible from any point in the room — the ruling spirit of the place. More on display, I'm sure, than you'd ever care to be. And you probably won't like it that I hung both the Chinese landscape and the Rouault on the front wall of the living room, one on each side of the doorway. Too much like an art gallery for you. But for me, those uncluttered surfaces of your Regency striped wallpaper always made the place feel a bit chilly (and empty), as if we were on the verge of moving. And ever since you've been gone, the feeling's been even worse. So, the artwork is keeping me company, especially the hanging, which reminds me of that day at the art institute in Chongqing, when you were so set upon buying it that you wouldn't consider any of the others. What was it, I wonder, that caught your eye — you never explained your attraction to it — the height of the mountain, the vividness of the waterfall, or the two diminutive people near the bottom, so dwarfed by the landscape that I never noticed them until today?

WEDNESDAY, JULY 23

Dear Kate,

Here it is, eight months since you died, and I'm still trying to keep in touch, bringing you back to life through words alone. A life after death in language. An absurd project, you might say, but a life in words is more durable than flesh and blood. And now that I've been writing you for so long, it almost feels like telling you of my days in days gone by, though I don't mention it to others, unless they ask me, "Are you still writing her?" And then I nod but don't say much in return. What could I possibly say? "I'm still doing it, but not as often as before"? As if it were a bad habit? Or, "Now that I've been doing it so long, I don't know how to stop without feeling that I've abandoned her forever." As if I'd completely taken leave of my senses. Actually, I sometimes think that I've become a grief specialist of sorts, thanks to all that I've written about me and my grieving. Writing, after all, is a way of learning, as I used to tell my students, so who could possibly claim to know more about grief than me? I've got eight months of letters to prove it. Letters that have helped me track the ups and downs of my anguish, like the highs and lows of my pulse and blood pressure during a cardiovascular stress test. I see now how labile it is from day to day, week to week, month to month — how it besets me less often than before, but no less suddenly and unpredictably. I see, in other words, that I'm getting better, as the saying goes, but I also realize that I will probably never be cured. Does anyone ever get over such a loss, or is it like a permanent malady, like another kind of heart disease from the one that I already have? And the best thing to do is learn how to live with it. So I keep on writing, hoping one day that I'll know so much I can stop going to school. Until then, the memories of you that words call forth are enough to sustain me, especially when I remember you back in the 1970s, bent over your tablet at the dining room table, penning your plays day in, day out, with nothing to sustain you but the words themselves, calling forth life in the wake of Sarah's death — your sister blown to smithereens in a mountainside airline crash and you here with nothing to do but receive the remains and piece things together in language.

FRIDAY, JULY 25

Dear Kate,

When it rains, it pours, or so it seems after the saga of the last three days. Actually, it started with the Sunday night downpour, which not only damaged the art shots but also drenched the stairway carpeting so heavily that it started to smell a few days ago, and the smell turned bad enough that I called a carpet cleaner, who washed it from top to bottom, sprayed it with a deodorant, put a fan at the base of the steps and assured me that "the deodorant smell will be gone in two or three days, and let's hope the smell of your carpet is gone too. It smells like a dog must have gone there in years past, and you probably tried to wash it off, but the residue was waiting like a time bomb, and there's nothing like water to set if off." So, our dear departed Pip is still here in his fashion. No wonder Puck was frantic when he first smelled it, running back and forth as if some other critter had marked his territory, whereas I thought at first that he might have marked it himself. Then after the carpet cleaner left, I was running back and forth to see if the smell had disappeared, but the sickly sweet deodorant was so strong I began to worry about it too. You, of course, had such a good nose for things you'd probably have been able to sniff out the difference. You also had such a sensitive nose that by that point you'd probably have been clamoring to rip out the carpet and start all over again. Which is what I decided to do yesterday after Holly came over to sniff it and recommended Patty, a carpet specialist, who also sniffed it and delivered her verdict. "It's beautiful carpeting — hard to believe that it's thirty years old, but that smell is bad, real bad, and there's no telling what it's like in the padding. If it were my home, I'd have it ripped out before it gets any worse." And that's what happened this morning, when she sent out Don, who went about his business in the methodical style of a native Iowan, and a half hour later the pine steps were completely bare, glowing almost as brightly as when you had them varnished some thirty-three years ago. Don, as you might imagine, had little to say, except for his admiration of the woodwork, so I told him how all the trim was covered with ten coats of paint when we bought the place, and that you and Martha spent the whole summer stripping it off and varnishing the wood before we moved in. That brought a twinkle to his eye, and then he was on his way, after giving me a piece of the old carpet for comparison with the new samples.

Casting my eye over a full spectrum of colors on one of the sample boards, I noticed an off- pink that nearly matched the color of our couch as well as some of the decorative figures in the oriental rug. Why not try something different, I thought, especially if it's coordinated with colors in the living room? And that's how I spent most of the afternoon, pondering the choice of a livelier green or an off-pink, moving the samples up and down the stairs, as you might have done, until I settled on the green when I noticed that the pink seemed a bit bland and washed out by comparison. It's only stairway carpeting, but I sure wish you were making the choice rather than me.

SATURDAY, JULY 26
Dear Kate,

Alan called a few days ago to invite me for dinner this evening, and without even thinking, the words came out of my mouth — "I'm busy," I said, and that was that. Yet I couldn't help wondering what had gotten into me, to fib my way out of a dinner invitation, especially with longtime friends like Alan and Kris. I've never done such a thing before. So I asked Carol about it when I saw her at the co-op today, and she told me straight out, "You've got to trust your feelings. I certainly did after Pierre died. Just think how long you and Kate were together, how accustomed you were to going places with her, and it's not surprising that you might be reluctant to go somewhere without her, even to be with people you know quite well, like Alan and Kris." A plausible enough explanation — until this afternoon, when the new issue of *Saveur* arrived, with such an enticing feature on Sardinia and Sardinian cooking that I called Trudy in New Jersey and asked if she'd like to go there sometime next year. I didn't ask her right off, of course — not until we brought each other up to date on our various maladies. But none of her problems deterred me from the thought of Sardinia, and they evidently didn't discourage her either — "I've always wanted to go there, but never did when I was living in Italy. Yes, oh yes, let's go — next year sounds great!" Well, it sounded great to me too, until I began to think about my erratic behavior — not wanting to go to dinner or anywhere else without you, but eager to go to Sardinia with Trudy after telling myself (and others) that I didn't know whether I'd ever feel like traveling again without you. No wonder people say you should wait a year before making any big decisions.

SUNDAY, JULY 27
Dear Kate,

Talk about life-altering decisions — I made one of those a few days ago, but didn't want to say anything until I was confident of being able to follow through on it. It happened last Wednesday at David's, where I went for dinner and noticed that he and Rebecca looked somewhat thinner than when I saw them a month or two ago, which made me wonder if they'd been dieting, or if something else was at work. I was curious because I've overeaten so much since you died that I now weigh more than two hundred pounds — 205 as of a few days ago. "The great rotundity," as you used to call it, is greater than ever before. Bad news not only for my heart but also my back, my knees, and everything else. A few weeks ago, in fact, the orthopedist gave me a handout noting that people who weigh over 205 are especially prone to suffer the pain of severe osteoarthritis in their knees and other weight-bearing joints. But the message itself was not so convincing as the pain — as you always said, there's nothing like pain to make a believer of me. So the thought of being able to get rid of it through a more-or-

less painless diet made me wonder what was up with David and Rebecca. And sure enough, they've been on a high protein—low carbo-
hydrate diet. Plus exercise. So that, in a nutshell, is what I decided to
do, starting Thursday morning with a two-mile walk before breakfast.
And I've kept to it for four straight days, which makes me think I can
do it from here on out, though I sure do miss the wine and the pasta.
On the other hand, the fruits and veggies are so good right now that
it's almost painless. And the pain in my knees is almost gone, which is
certainly cause for celebration. Why, then, did I suddenly find myself
in tears when I was thinking of you late this afternoon? Maybe it was a
fleeting remembrance of the day you died and your last words, "You'll
take care of the rice, won't you? And the lamb too?" Or perhaps it was
a fleeting dream of you this morning, the first in several weeks, a dream
in which I was looking at a few mementos of our life together, broke
into tears, then asked you if it was always that way, and you said, matter of factly, "That's what I understand, that's the way it goes."

THURSDAY, AUGUST 7

Dear Kate,

This afternoon, I had lunch with Jean, an energetic woman I met a
few years ago when she was volunteering at the animal shelter. She
asked me over to meet a nonfiction writer on his way to Montana, but
his story was nothing compared to Jean's recollection of her husband's
death several years ago. It all came out when she asked if I'm writing
anything special, and I told her about these letters, which led her into
such a disturbing account that I'll never forget it. Partly, I suppose, it
was the fearful symmetry that got me — her husband suddenly swept
away in an afternoon, in three hours, just like you, without any premonition, just like you, at Mercy Hospital, just like you, despite her immediately having called 911, just like me. But even as I was stunned by
the symmetry, I was appalled by the harrowing difference. For while
you died of an irreversibly fatal hemorrhage, he suffered a heart attack
that might not have been fatal had the paramedics not lingered in his
university hospital office for fifteen minutes, checking symptoms and
asking where he wanted to be taken — and had he, a doctor, not asked
to be cared for at Mercy rather than the emergency room of the hospital where he was already located. What if, I kept wondering to my-

self, as I listened to her story, especially because she too still seemed to be wondering what if. But the thing that got me more than anything else were the questions she asked me — "Did you think she would die when it started to happen? Did you think she would die when the ambulance came so quick? Did you think she would die when you first got to the hospital?" Denial, it seems, is in the nature of things, for the thought never entered my mind until the doctor put it there shortly after I first saw you in the emergency room, barely conscious, and he told me you might not survive. His words were like a bombshell. But in Jean's case, the thought hardly crossed her mind while she sat in the waiting room for three hours, only to be told after the fact that her husband had died. No wonder she spoke of having wailed and wailed — involuntary keening. No wonder she's still beset by the memory of that terrible afternoon. But now she also speaks of being blessed with pleasant dreams, dreams of traveling with him. Which made me think that perhaps I should reprogram myself to dream of our travels, a trip beyond compare.

FRIDAY, AUGUST 15

Extra, extra, read all about it! I sold all your real-estate stock after talking with Sue, who assured me there'd be enough left over after taxes to double your initial investment, just as you wanted. Enough for a lavish gift to each of your nieces and nephews. The minute she gave me the good news, I told her, "Sell it all, all of it, while we've still doubled the money, 'cause that's what Kate wanted to do, and we've done it much sooner than she ever imagined." I remember your being so upset by the three-year decline that I thought you'd be elated by the nine-month turnaround. Now I wonder what you'd think if you knew it had tripled just three weeks ago, and that I held on hoping it might even quadruple by now. Talk about pipe dreams! And to what end, without you to enjoy it? Still, it's a rare thing to double one's money in just nine months. A gestation of sorts that should bring a few smiles to your nieces and nephews.

As for me, I was all smiles this afternoon when the pavers showed up to replace our dusty gravel with a new asphalt driveway, so deftly graded and edged that it looks like an exquisite work of industrial art, sweeping upward from the street, its jet black surface a striking contrast to the lush green lawn. So pristine that I fretted about it all afternoon, worrying even about the grass clippings from Brad's late-afternoon mowing. Maybe I should just ignore it, turn my back on it, go somewhere in the house where I can't see it and can't worry about its being marred. But what's the good of a new asphalt driveway if you can't admire it, can't eyeball it from top to bottom and side to side, can't hose it down to cool the surface and wash away the leaves, the grass clippings, the footprints, the dust in the air? What's the good of it if you can't share the news of it with your one true love? Extra, extra, read all about it!

SUNDAY, AUGUST 17

Dear Kate,

So many ripe tomatoes on the vines that I decided to make a batch of your favorite sauce with garlic, chopped onion, fresh oregano, and basil. *Salsa pizzaiola!* No sweat, thought I — just harvest the ingredients, follow the recipe in the Time-Life Italian cookbook, stir things up in the big black pot, and freeze the sauce in plastic containers. The only problem is that the book and the pot turned out to be time bombs. First it was the recipe page, penned with your handwritten annotations, discolored with age, torn from the spiral binder, like a relic of your summer days. Then it was the big pot that I haven't used since you died, with the smaller one nested inside of it. So many sauces and soups and stews therein that I wept like a child at the thought of all the labor and love that went into them. No coarse sauces for you, like the one I made today. Nothing less than a fine purée would do. And you never stopped cooking like that, never stopped feeling like that, never stopped being yourself, right up to your last words about the rice and lamb. The mere thought of those words and your constancy makes me wonder about the state of my own feelings. So variable and inconstant I often feel guilty that my grief is not as frequent or pervasive as it was several months go. An outburst today, but nothing the week before, and then only when I looked at your recipe for scaloppini olé, as if your cooking were the only thing that rouses me these days. When I told that to Connie this evening, she said, "You can't keep grieving the way you did in December, you just can't. And even if you could, it wouldn't be healthy." I couldn't disagree, but still it sometimes seems like a terrible betrayal. Something is taking its course, and I don't feel good about it.

WEDNESDAY, AUGUST 20

Dear Kate,

So hot and humid the past few weeks that I got my hair cut short this morning, then took Puck into the groomer's for the same thing, and now he looks more comfortable than he has all summer. Too bad, though, that he wasn't around when Jean called, inviting him to meet her border collie and romp in her fenced backyard. But our dogs were the least of it. No sooner did we finish chatting about collies and terriers than we were talking again about her husband's death and yours, how nothing prepared us for the suddenness and swiftness. The shock so terrible it left us both more dazed and devastated than we had ever been before, more vulnerable than anyone could possibly imagine who hadn't suffered such a thing themselves. We talked like members of an exclusive club, open only to persons afflicted by the grief of sudden death. A rare bond, a camaraderie extraordinaire. Our pain so far beyond the ken of others that we mocked their cheery greetings, their hopeful questions. How naive of them to think we could ever feel as good as their cheeriness implied, as if "closure," that god-awful word of our time, were truly possible. But while we were in mocking mode, I couldn't help noticing the cheeriness of her voice, especially compared to my own somber tones. And I wondered if it was her native Irish buoyancy — the irrepressible lilt in her voice — or the passage of several years since her husband's death, or a deliberate attempt to be of good cheer. Whatever the cause, it made me think that while I might never get over your death, I could learn how to live with it or at least contrive to put a good face on things, like hers.

THURSDAY, AUGUST 21

Dear Kate,

This evening I decided to put on my cheeriest face for Holly and Becky, who came over for dinner just when a cool breeze wafted in, so I was actually feeling cheerier than I had all day. They, in turn, were coming for their monthly cheering session, so we were a terminally cheery threesome. We dined on the terrace — my showpiece a platter of the gulf shrimp that you bought and froze last November. And a batch of your piquant seafood sauce. Holly thought they were "perfect," and Becky said they were "the best shrimp" she ever had. So, your bounty is still gracing the dinner table. And your writing is still food for thought, as I discovered when Holly showed me a favorable review of your "Chemo-Log," noting in particular your frank reporting, your lively prose, your gritty details, your staunch outlook. I gave her a copy several months ago, on the chance that the press might be interested in publishing it. The only problem is that the reviewer made several suggestions for revising and updating the manuscript, which of course you're not in a position to do. And I don't think you'd be inclined to make the changes even if you could, since revisions would force you to polish an account that you evidently wanted to leave untouched, as a reflection of the way you were affected by the chemo. Talk about putting a good face on things.

SATURDAY, AUGUST 23

Dear Kate,

Today is the nine-month anniversary of your death, a complete gestation period, and I didn't give birth to anything but four jars of kosher dills, a faceful of tears, and this letter. How strange that a nine-month anniversary should be such a big deal as to make me more vulnerable than I've been the past several months. But that's what happened when I stopped at Holly's new house to see how the construction is going and she asked me how I'm doing. It's been a long time since I broke down in front of someone. But her innocent question suddenly made me feel your absence and my loneliness more intensely than I could bear. I guess it was the image of her making a new home that got to me, a painful reminder of the summer you were making one for us. And all day after my visit to Holly, I kept reliving the day of your death until the exact time of it at ten of five, when I was distracted by driving across town for a picnic at David and Rebecca's. I picked up Carol on the way over, and it was good to have such an understanding companion. For a while at least, the party was also a pleasant distraction, until the crush of people was more than I could bear. Maybe Bacon was right — that "a crowd is not company, faces are but a gallery of pictures, and talk but a tinkling cymbal, where there is no love."

SATURDAY, AUGUST 30

Dear Kate,

We're now in the sixth week of a sustained heat wave and drought, a striking reversal of the cool, wet weather that lasted through mid-July. How beguiling it was back then to behold the verdant lawn, the florid growth in your perennial bed, the bumper yields in my vegetable plots, and imagine that we might get through an entire summer without having to water. Now, I'm beginning to wonder if it'll ever rain again, especially after a week of lugging the hose from bed to bed, and nightly predictions of rain that come to naught. Nothing, of course, is forever, but a sustained run of things, one way or the other, sure does have an aura of invincibility. I was thinking about that today, when I realized that a week had gone by without my shedding a tear. I too am having a drought of sorts, though I'll probably have rain soon enough, given our wedding anniversary next week. In the meantime, I've been getting a boost every time I go upstairs or down and eyeball the new carpeting that was installed a few days ago. It appears to be the same color as before, which goes so well with the wallpaper and the wood that I can see why you chose it. But the thing that really gave me a boost was a visit to the nursery this morning, where I bought ten large chrysanthemums for your perennial bed. Once the drought is over, I'll put them in along the front for some more touches of fall color — three yellow at each end, four lavender along the center. Given your fondness for mums, I trust you approve.

TUESDAY, SEPTEMBER 2

Dear Kate,

The drought finally ended two days ago, and I followed suit yesterday afternoon with a downpour of my own, thanks to a note from Elizabeth, thanking me for the wedding gift I sent her a few weeks ago — a cut-glass flower vase — "It looks exactly like something that Aunt Kate would have chosen." And indeed it does, because I had in mind the cut-glass vase that you picked out when your brother got married some thirty-five years ago. Like parents, like daughter. I forgot to tell you that she's getting married in a couple of weeks, and I'm planning to attend with Martha, so at least a couple of us will be there from your side of the family. Maybe I wouldn't have been so touched by Elizabeth's note if I hadn't also been thinking of our own anniversary today, or if Martha hadn't called a few minutes later, to confirm our travel arrangements for the wedding. So many connubial thoughts and memories converging just then, it was more than I could handle. After yesterday's breakdown, I wonder what I'll be like at the wedding itself. But at least it left me dry-eyed today, which I spent in the garden pulling weeds, pondering again your words on our drought-ridden thirtieth anniversary — "These are the flowers that we have. We don't have the others, so there's no point in talking about them." I couldn't help wondering if you'd still give me that stern advice, as if to suggest I should stop thinking about you, stop writing about you, stop living in the past. So I tried to imagine what it would be like to forget you, to put you out of mind, to erase you from the tablets of my memory. Such a daunting thought problem that I didn't even know how to begin thinking about it, much less how to forget. And it didn't help come dinner, when I opened a bottle of the pinot noir we discovered on the way to Mendocino and remembered the morning we drove north-northwest through the Anderson Valley, toward that rocky seacoast town, you at the wheel, the road twisting and turning through a foggy landscape that suddenly cleared off just when we were approaching the vineyard of our dreams, the pinot noir of our desires. A heady reminder, as if I needed one, that all the roads I take lead back to you.

SUNDAY, SEPTEMBER 7

Dear Kate,

I've been out of touch for a few days, thanks to a weekend visit by Nancy. A surprise that unfolded several weeks ago, when she sent a generous gift to your memorial fund and an invitation to visit her in Manhattan. I replied with an invitation to come here, and lo! she took me up on the offer. How strange to see her outside of our editorial get-togethers in Boston and New York. But I guess she knows what I've been going through, given the loss of her husband, whom she talked about so vividly that he might have been dead just a year or two rather than a quarter century or more. Which made me wonder how I might be talking of you if I live that much longer — into my nineties, for God's sake! But it was certainly clear from everything she said that Nancy admired your frankness, your edginess, given a razor-sharp tongue of her own. I especially liked her parting advice when I took her to the airport this morning — "Beware of widders bearing meat-loaves!" No wonder she brought a bottle of rioja. But how about this? That tongue of hers was hardly in evidence all weekend long, and the same for her eastern seaboard airs. Au contraire, she sounded more like a nostalgic daughter, when I took her out to Lake Macbride for a walk along the shore, and asked her what it was like growing up in the same town where E. B. White was born and raised. Once more to the lake, in her own vein, and when she wasn't reminiscing about Mount Vernon, she was telling me about her daughters and grandchildren. How surprising, to think of her as a woman with family, with attachments and affections, when I've always thought of her the past twenty years as a collaborator, academician, and administrator par excellence. And it wasn't just that afternoon, but all the next day when we were getting things ready for a dinner party on the terrace, and then she was almost like a wife, gently but firmly taking things in hand (or taking me in hand), suggesting that we get the car washed, and the ice cube trays filled, and the kitchen floor vacuumed, and the table set just so, as if I hadn't already spruced things up enough for guests. Then for a moment, it felt so much like you that I was suddenly moved to give her one of your necklaces. With a tailored shirt like one of yours, she could have passed for a sister, or a cousin at least. I wonder what she was thinking just then, but she didn't let on. And that was that, though we certainly did turn a few heads at a museum opening the night before. So from start to finish, it was a delightful weekend, a gift from one widder to another.

SUNDAY, SEPTEMBER 14

Dear Kate,

Nothing of note the past several days, except for a fishing jaunt yesterday morning in the middle of an intermittent rainstorm. But how could I refuse an invitation from Will — son of my dear, departed colleague Bob, the most dapper and courtly man I've ever known, who kept me sane before you came upon the scene. Will's in town for John's memorial service this afternoon, so yesterday's rainy adventure was like another memorial of sorts for John and Bob and others from our fishing group of yore. Will's so elegant a flycaster, like his father, that I couldn't help thinking of Bob as we tried the shoreline, bluegills snapping at our bugs from time to time but nothing large enough to keep. I was thinking just then of how Bob taught me to flycast some forty years ago — "It's all in the wrist," he said — and also explained how to survive the divorce from Meredith — "It's all in the forgetting," he said, recalling how he'd survived his own. So I was wondering what he might have taught me this time around, especially when I remembered how you and I had walked that shore just a year ago, Puck on the leash, tugging as if he knew exactly where we were headed, and you making fun of his headstrong way, as if either of us knew what lay ahead.

How blithe we were back then, a thought that came to mind after Connie called this morning, wanting to know the exact time of John's memorial, and then told me about touring his house a few weeks ago with someone from the Writers' Workshop who's interested in buying it. The thought of them going through his place, site of all those joyous dinners and department parties, suddenly made me realize that it's now completely empty — the furniture, the paintings, the books, all the marks of his living there for more than fifty years, all gone as surely as he. An emblem of things to come here on Reno Street. How strange that I hadn't ever thought of its being empty, though he died almost three months ago. Talk about being in denial! And it was the same with Carol, when I told her about it at lunch today — she too was surprised, though God knows she of all people should have realized the dismantling that would take place in the wake of his death. She visited him so often during the years of his decline that you'd think she'd have known what was coming. But even she was blindsided by the inevitable. How strange, given the eloquent memory of John that she shared at the service, a memory from one of their last excursions when he suddenly gave voice to a haunting line from *Huckleberry Finn* — "They swum by, they slid along so quiet and smooth and lovely," as if he were bearing witness to how the best moments of our lives (how all the days of our lives) swim by us without our knowing they're irretrievably past.

TUESDAY, SEPTEMBER 16

Dear Kate,

The radishes I planted on Friday have already broken ground, as I discovered this morning when I went out to seed in some arugula. Wouldn't it be nice if the rest of life were as easy as radishes? I also thought about doing some kale and turnips, but without you to savor them, it seemed like a waste of good seed. Besides, I got a bushel of tomatoes on the vine, a host of ripening peppers, and no signs of frost in the offing. So balmy today that Carol put together a picnic basket, and we lunched at Kent Park, while Puck took the breeze on a stake-out. Driving through a grove of trees, she remarked on "the color and light this time of year." I didn't say anything, lest I burden her with an emotional outburst. But her remark reminded me of what Trudy said last week when I told her the tears have been coming again. "It's probably the change of seasons," she said, "the coming of fall." Trudy's remark didn't make sense just then, because it didn't seem as if fall had yet arrived, and the thought of its arrival didn't yet weigh heavy on my mind. But now that your favorite season is here — in the crisp morning air, the yellowing walnut leaves, the slant of the sun in the southern sky — it's no wonder I'm having trouble again. Especially when I think of how it was some thirty-six years ago this fall, a few weeks after we were married, visiting your Uncle Buck and Aunt Kay, who beamed at you, then proudly declared that "Kate is a child of fall. You can see it in her coloring and the colors she's wearing." Those colors are beginning to return again, and their return, I now see, is breaking my heart.

FRIDAY, SEPTEMBER 19

Dear Kate,

Elizabeth's wedding takes place tomorrow, so I flew to Denver this afternoon. Martha was waiting for me in the baggage claim area, looking as usual like a dark-haired, sun-tanned version of you — all smiles that our prearranged meeting place worked out. And a bigger smile when we entered our sumptuous room at the top of the Brown Palace, its tall windows looking directly out to the front range of the Rockies. And the biggest smile of all when I gave her your mother-of-pearl brooch, its circular shape and silver setting a perfect match for her new

Chinese-style outfit. But that was nothing compared to the look on Elizabeth's face and then the tears and then the big, big hug when I gave her your long pearl necklace at the groom's dinner and told her that the last time you wore it was at her brother's wedding. I also gave her a picture of you wearing the pearls at his wedding, then draped them around her in exactly the same way — a small circle around the neck, the rest hanging down to her waist. So striking that she glittered the rest of the evening. And I felt glittery too with the satisfaction of being a sugar daddy of sorts. But I didn't know quite how to feel when people came up and told me, "You look so good, you really look good," with a genuine air of surprise in their voice. Did they expect me to look disheveled, as if grief had completely undone me? Au contraire, I bought myself two new shirts for the occasion that go perfectly with my silk jacket. So, with a twinkle in my eye, I hope, I told them that "Kate always said a little suffering is good for one's looks.'"

SATURDAY, SEPTEMBER 20

Dear Kate,

From start to finish, the wedding was so beautiful that it cast the rest of this lovely day in the shade. Fresh air, mountain vistas, blue skies, glassy skyscrapers — nothing could compete, not even the Denver Art Museum's striking exhibit of Northwest Indian culture, totems, tents, and all. A special treat for Martha, given her Indian-inspired art. But even she was swept away by the church where the wedding took place. A turn-of-the-century stone edifice, with an off-center spire, its stained glass windows, blue, blue, blue, glowed in the late afternoon sun. Glowed even in the shade of downtown office buildings. And so did the rich brown marble interior, the decoratively carved wood above the altar, the cross-shaped chandeliers. Such a gorgeous place we couldn't stop gawking. But it wasn't just the church that entranced me — also the string trio, punctuating the ceremony with Vivaldi, Pachelbel, Bach, Handel, and Schubert. And the homily was an eloquent celebration of love, thanks to the resonant Irish brogue of the Jesuit father who delivered it and to his impassioned knowledge of bride and groom. They, of course, were the star attraction and delivered their lines with the assurance of experienced performers. Yet they played their parts — kneeling, standing, facing each other, exchanging rings, holding and kissing each other — with the freshness and delicacy of shy young lovers. When they stood facing the priest, I noticed for the first time that the bottom of Elizabeth's floor-length veil was edged with lace flowers from the surplus of your veil that I'd given her at the memorial service, but completely forgotten until she turned around, and there were the flowers trailing behind her. So lovely to see them again, it almost soothed the sting of seeing your name on the back of the program, in memory of relatives "no longer with us." How strange to see you side by side with sister Sarah, gone some thirty years ago. You shared a bedroom growing up, and now you share a line of type. An inky cohabitation. Not exactly the troth you plighted, but better, I suppose, than nothing. As for me, this evening's destination was the top of the Qwest Building, otherwise known as the Pinnacle Club — not exactly the apex of my dreams, but I could hardly complain, given the ample champagne, the front range, the tornadic sky, and the buoyant newlyweds.

MONDAY, SEPTEMBER 22

Dear Kate,

Yesterday morning, I broke the fast with Martha and a Rocky Mountain trout in the Brown Palace dining room, and this morning — oh, modern life! — I was back here at sea level in the hearing-aid clinic, where Diane gave me such a frank assessment of my hearing problems that her words are still ringing in my ears. Though I was there to pick up a repaired hearing aid, I also asked if she could fit me with a more powerful set of aids, for the ones I've been using the past three years don't seem quite as helpful as before. That's when she gave me such an earful, it sounded as if she'd been lying in wait. "I'm not sure that you need a new pair of hearing aids. And I certainly couldn't advise you to make such a decision without having an up-to-date test of your hearing. Besides, you should realize that your personal situation has changed so much since Kate died that there's no telling how it might have affected your hearing or your perception of it. After all, you're talking and listening to different people than before, and that's bound to make a difference." Which put me in mind of that old love song, "I Only Have Eyes for You," but in a new vein, "I only have ears for you." Perhaps that's why I've been having trouble with others. Hearing Diane hold forth, her voice as clear as it's always been, I suddenly remembered how strong your voice was, and how you always spoke loudly and clearly enough for me to hear you, oh public speaker of yore, and I in turn didn't hesitate to ask that you repeat yourself, especially when I was in the attic and you on the first floor. But that's not always the way things go with others, particularly folks whose voice is too soft, or twangy, or accented, or otherwise indecipherable. Sometimes they don't take the trouble, and neither do I. I only have ears for you.

TUESDAY, SEPTEMBER 23

Dear Kate,

Trudy called this morning with the extraordinary news that she's been given a Whiting Award — as in thirty-five thousand big ones — for her essay collection that Holly and I just published this fall. A wonderful and well-deserved honor, which reminded me of your enthusiasm for the pieces when you read them last fall. What you didn't know back then was that she had dedicated the tree essay to you, but I didn't tell you, because she wanted it to be a surprise. So much for surprises. I'm also not supposed to tell anyone about the award until it's publicly announced in New York at the end of October, but I figured it would be safe to let you in on the news.

Speaking of good news, today's mail brought a batch of slides from Hannah of her most recent artwork — a multimedia series featuring an alchemist's vessel in each of twenty-two separate pictures that combine painting and collage set against a gold background, inscribed with Hannah's handwritten meditations. Variations on a theme that she explained in an accompanying statement about the alchemy of human relationships — a transforming process in which "the fire of love" turns "the base metal of whoever we are into something entirely fine and different." I was so moved by the thought, as well as by the entire series, that I called her this evening to talk about it, to see if she might be interested in a local exhibit, and to buy two of the pieces myself. It's not that I need any more pictures anywhere in the house. It's just that the images are so evocative — one with a flame inside the vessel and the hint of a human figure inside the flame, the other with a vividly blue butterfly emerging from the vessel — that they make me think of you and the alchemy of your love. Hannah and I talked about all the pictures in such detail that only afterward did I realize how clear her voice was from start to finish, which made me think that perhaps I don't need a new pair of hearing aids after all. Maybe I just needed to have the one repaired, the other cleared of wax, and care enough to hear the very best.

WEDNESDAY, SEPTEMBER 24

Dear Kate,

Not until today did I realize that the ten-month anniversary of your death was yesterday. And I only realized it when I was lunching on the terrace with Kären and Margaret of the Iowa Women's Archive, telling them about the day you died. Margaret had written me last month about acquiring your papers — "She was one strong, creative Iowa woman; we would like to preserve her legacy." So I had them over to see what you created here at home, apart from your writing, park planning, and tree saving. But the pleasant get-together suddenly turned strange when I realized yesterday's oversight. From that point on, I could hardly keep my mind on them and my story. Talk about a schizoid experience — I've never experienced anything quite like it. There I was calmly telling them about the afternoon you died, bemused by the calmness of my tale, when the realization of yesterday's anniversary threw me into a panic, and then into a bizarre internal dialogue, berating myself for the oversight and then for the panic itself, while also trying to keep up the genial surface of a polite host. I wonder if they noticed that I was there and not there. I wonder what they'd have said if I had told them what I was going through right then, and that it was all the result of an innocent question by Margaret — "Were there any premonitions of what happened that day?" But now that I'm sitting here at the kitchen table, pondering that moment in the solitude of evening, I can't help feeling grateful for her question, since it ultimately led me to realize that I'm not keeping track anymore. Or not keeping track every month in that compulsive way of mine. I'm not even keeping track of things day by day anymore, though every day in its way is an anniversary of your death. But their visit also led me to see that it's time to start letting go of things. So before they left, I gave them all your modeling shots and proof sheets, and in the months to come I'll give them your letters, your manuscripts, your drawings and draftings, for they can preserve such things far better than I.

FRIDAY, SEPTEMBER 26

Dear Kate,

Yesterday morning I got a call from the friendly skies of United, informing me that the first leg of my flight to Hawaii had been rescheduled to such an ungodly hour — six in the morning, meaning check-in at five — that I revised the whole flight plan for a later departure and a different set of flights. A simple enough matter, it seemed, until I tried to do the same thing for Trudy and was told that I couldn't reschedule her ticket, since it was booked through a travel agent. So I called Trudy, who called her travel agent, who called United, and that was just the beginning of an all-day game of phone tag that ended today, with Trudy and me rebooked on the same flights, but only after such a byzantine runaround that she blew off the friendly skies, and I almost did the same, wondering again, as I did back in May, if the trip is so ill-fated that I should scatter your ashes in the Iowa River rather than lugging them all the way to Hanalei Bay. Sometimes I wonder what's gotten into me that I cling so fiercely to that faraway place. Especially since you didn't ask and I didn't promise to scatter you there. But then again, I can't help remembering what you said last fall when we were planning our spring return. I had just spoken of it as "the most beautiful place I could ever imagine," and you suddenly turned from the kitchen counter, looked me squarely in the eye, and calmly said, "For me it's a place of spiritual renewal." And that was that.

SUNDAY, SEPTEMBER 28

Dear Kate,

Ever since you died, I've been tantalized by glimmerings about the mystery of things — and frustrated by my inability to put them into words. Better I should leave such things to seers and mystics, you'd probably say. Or cosmic theorists and evolutionary biologists. But the glimmerings keep coming, especially now that the leaves are turning, the age-old cycle completing another round. The sap rising, the sap falling. The trees seemingly dying off, shedding their leaves like reckless spenders, only to be reborn come spring and prove mysterious in their lavish ways. But not half so miraculous as our coming to consciousness — our thoughts, our feelings, the very ground of our being so familiar, so compelling, that it seems as if we, our selves, are as tangible, as palpable, as our bodily parts, though in fact we're nothing more or less than an extension of our brain. "An emergent property," according to the jargon of scientists, as Trudy told me the other day when she was trying to help me make sense of my glimmerings and puzzlings. "That's the way they refer to something that's greater than the sum of its parts, like life arising from a bunch of chemicals, or consciousness from flesh and blood alone. The existence of it can't really be accounted for." So it's all the more mysterious, though usually taken so for granted in the ordinary run of experience, that only when it's suddenly swept away, as swiftly as you were, does one realize how extraordinary it really is. And how incredibly evanescent. Here one moment, gone the next. That's what keeps haunting me about our last few minutes together in the kitchen, when you were so exuberant about the bowls and jewelry you'd just bought — so full of thought and feeling as you talked about your purchases and the art fair and the dinner party — that it seemed as if you were at the height of your powers, in the summer of your life. And then suddenly you were evanescing before my very eyes, disappearing as mysteriously as you had come into being. From summer to fall to winter in the sweep of those expressions across your face. And no chance of spring, of our eyes making contact again. On the other hand, the daffodils you planted some thirty falls ago bloomed again last spring along the south lot line — hundreds of them now from a few dozen of them back then. And for all I know they might bloom there for thirty more years, and thirty more again. The work of your hands returning every spring, thousands by then from a few dozen. Now, of course, they're invisible, having died back last June, so it seems like a miracle to think of them blooming and multiplying year after year, world without end.

WEDNESDAY, OCTOBER 1

Dear Kate,

Today was the climax of a pre-frost frenzy that started on Sunday, when the meteorologists predicted overnight temperatures in the low thirties. In other words, a frost advisory. Once again the annual panic attack, then the second-guessing — denial always in the wings, especially with the first temperature drop. Then the fudging — how low is low? How low on our high ground? And then, of course, the usual precautions, row covers and all, draping this, wrapping that — Cristo in the garden. All day Sunday I tucked things in, not even breaking for Miriam's New Year's party. Such a tedious, compulsive, and ultimately fruitless task, I couldn't help asking myself the perennial question — why not harvest the tender crops, pick the vulnerable flowers, and get on with the season? But even you couldn't resist the urge to sustain things, asking me to drape your stuff as well as mine. At first I thought it was just a natural desire to keep things flowering and ripening another week or two or more. Yet the longer I tried to keep things going, the more it seemed like a competitive thing. The macho gardener, strutting his stuff with tomatoes in November, lettuce in December, radishes in January, leeks in February. I've strutted so many times, though, that now I see it's deeper down than that, especially after last fall, especially with a killing frost in the low twenties predicted for tomorrow. Lower than anything on record for that date. So severe that not even the row covers will suffice. Nothing to do, then, but acknowledge the inevitable — in the garden as in life itself. No emergency room measures. No delays. No palliatives. So it was a day of harvest and then farewell to the plants. Talk about fall! Now it's definitely here.

THURSDAY, OCTOBER 2

Dear Kate,

Off and on since you died, I've thought about getting a cellphone for the car, in case of emergencies. But I've always been put off by memories of the one we had several years ago — so difficult for me to hear that I could hardly believe your ability to use it. Today, though, I was shopping at the mall, came upon a cellphone store, and there all my suppositions were reversed. For no sooner did I tell the clerk that I'm hard of hearing than he said, "I've got exactly what you're looking for. Just dial a number and listen to this!" Such an obvious sales pitch that I almost walked out then and there. But the sound of that little clamshell turned out to be as good as a corded phone — maybe even better. So how could I resist? Forty dollars a month for four hundred anytime-anywhere minutes, a thousand mobile-to-mobile minutes, and unlimited nighttime and weekend minutes — all of them audible! And other features galore! The only problem is that I've been obsessed with it ever since, charging its battery, trying it out in the car (parked, of course), programming all of its functions — its brightness, its contrast, its screen color, its ringer, its volume, its phonebook, even my own screen line, "Carl's Phone." Narcissus with a clamshell! I've tested its calculator, sampled its scheduler, tried out its voice dialer. And now I've decided to use it not only for all my long-distance calls but also on my exercise walks. I also intend to put it by my bedside, just in case I have to make an emergency call from there. I mean, how desperate can one get for companionship. If only it could put me in touch with you.

FRIDAY, OCTOBER 3

Dear Kate,

Thanks to all those anytime-anywhere minutes, I called Nancy this afternoon in Hanalei — I haven't been in touch with her since last January, and I wanted to be sure that everything is in order for the house and for scattering your ashes in the bay. Turns out she had just contacted her friend who captains the outrigger crew, and he'll take us on November 15 or 16, a Saturday or Sunday. Then I called Ruth, who's coming over from Oahu, to give her the dates. When I first met Ruth some twenty years ago, I never imagined that my visit to her campus in Honolulu would lead to our long-time love affair with Hawaii. I also never imagined that she'd outlive you, seeing as how she's almost old enough to be your mother. Ruth offered to consult her Hawaiian friend Pua about a special native prayer for the occasion. And that made me wonder what I might say (or pray) other than to bid you farewell and promise to join you when my ashes are scattered in the bay. Anything more would probably be too much for your taste and too long for me to get through without breaking down. The only remaining problem was how to transport your ashes, without their being confiscated as possible explosives. Talk about mistaken identity! And likely to happen, according to Amy, given the red-alert mindset of airport baggage checkers. Nancy suggested that I call the airline or ship them directly to her. But I didn't want to let them out of my hands, for fear of their being lost in transit. How's that for a postmodern burial? So I called the funeral home, and they'll not only give me a special letter of transit but also pack them safely for carrying in my shoulder bag. It never occurred to me that getting one's ashes from here to there could be such a complicated affair, but then again it never occurred to me that ashes could be mistaken for explosives.

MONDAY, OCTOBER 6

Dear Kate,

I've been trimming yews the past few days — snip-snip here, snip-snip there — watching their shape return as the overgrown leaders are pruned away. Once the sides are done, it's amusing to see their un-trimmed tops looking somewhat like a mohawk. Now I realize why you hand-trimmed them year after year, striving as you once told me to keep the cuts as hidden as possible. The secret art of pruning yews — without that hint, I'd not have been able to do them properly. But what will come of them when I'm gone? That question came to mind this morning, as I was reaching up to trim the top of a branch, and the answer was depressing, not because I'd be gone but because it didn't seem likely that anyone would bother to trim them by hand or even realize that they need it each year. At best, they might get shaved with a power clipper. And that gloomy supposition led me down an even more depressing path, as I imagined what would become of your perennial bed, my vegetable plots, and all the other plantings we've maintained here the past thirty-three years. Come to think of it, I'm not even sure how long I'll be able to maintain things myself, given my bum knees and the increasing height of the yews. But enough of such gloomy thoughts. The lawn right now is lushly green, the maple fiery red and orange, the walnuts pale yellow, the spindle trees cranberry, and your wild aster lavender, lavender. Just right for "a child in fall" to "spin and spin," as you said, "arms outflung, head thrown back, until creation whirls." Though I don't have the nerve (or verve) to spin right now, the yard itself is enough to make me dizzy.

WEDNESDAY, OCTOBER 8

Dear Kate,

I stopped at the workshop this morning to visit with Connie, and she asked how I'm doing, as she always does in her Sunday night calls. But talking with her in person this morning was a bit different from usual, for rather than being on the phone with a dear old friend, I was there in her office, and she was sitting behind her desk, Ben Franklins aslope on her nose, looking for all the world like a psychoanalyst rather than the workshop's administrative genius. So I answered her quite frankly, for she always has something wise or surprising to say in response. I told her how it's been harder than usual the past several weeks, and, like Trudy, she talked about seasonal change and the approaching anniversary of your death. Nothing surprising on that score, especially since I'm convinced that it also has something to do with the intense beauty of the changing leaves and the declining angle of the sun, lighting them up, heightening their color, but also heightening my sense of their imminent demise, about to be swept away as suddenly as you. So, when she asked me what was most upsetting, I told her it was the thought of your incredible loss, you who cherished life (and this gaudy season) more than anyone else I've ever known. And suddenly I was choking up, grieving for you, and that's when she took me by surprise, telling me flat out that "it's much harder for you than it was for her. She's gone and doesn't know what happened to her, so she's not really suffering, but you're still here, living with it every day. It's a harsh thing to say, but I worry more about the living than the dead." And that was also the brunt of what Carol said this afternoon when we were walking the shore of Lake Macbride. She didn't put it the same way as Connie, but when I told her that Hannah once thought I might be trying to hold on to you too tightly, she readily agreed and said that "letting go of her doesn't mean that you're forsaking her." True enough, but it's easier said than done.

FRIDAY, OCTOBER 10
Dear Kate,

Yesterday and today, I devoted myself to trimming the yews by the terrace. A solitary job with a satisfying payoff. Not the first time this year that I spent a day or two by myself and certainly not the last. But I've been thinking about it more than usual, thanks to a call from my brother. He began, as usual, by asking me how I'm doing, and "loneliness" was the word that suddenly came to mind, which led him to ask how many people I see each day. A strange question, I thought, as if to suggest that a people-filled life could make up for your absence. But I took the question seriously and replied with one of my own — "By 'people I see,' do you mean people I have lunch or dinner with or at least spend an hour or so talking with?" That being the case, I told him that I usually see no more than one or two a day and sometimes none. "That's not many people," he said, as swiftly as if he'd been lying in wait, and I suddenly felt so defensive that I asked him how many he sees each day. He paused a minute, and then admitted that he doesn't see any more than that himself, which moved me to suggest that perhaps we don't see many people because we're retired and therefore on the fringe of things.

But at dinner this evening, Carol said something about our marriage that made me see things in a different light, and not just because she said it so frankly, so bluntly, but also because it echoed something you said from time to time. "You and Kate," she said, "had such a loving and self-sufficient marriage that it sometimes seemed as if each of you and you alone were enough for the other, as if you didn't need the rest of the world for your happiness. And that was fine while both of you were alive, but it didn't really prepare either of you for the death of the other. So, in a way, it would have been better if both of you had died at the same time." How's that for a bold conclusion? So bold that even she looked a bit surprised when the words came out of her mouth. But the minute she said it, I remembered your occasional complaint that "we're too interdependent, too symbiotic," and I remembered as well the eerie experience of how you would sometimes voice an opinion or make an observation that was on the tip of my tongue, as if our brains were linked to each other. So I couldn't disagree about being ill prepared for your death. Ill prepared in more ways than one, especially given the utter surprise of it. But after a few moments of agreement, telling her what I've just said, it also seemed important to report all the things you taught me or inspired me to do, in the kitchen, in the house, in the garden, in my writing, in my life. So many things that it seems as if you'd been preparing me to survive without you — in every way but one.

SATURDAY, OCTOBER 11
Dear Kate,

Don and Ava came over for dinner this evening — he left D.C. this year to be a parttime lecturer here in the business school, and Ava's in town for a weeklong visit. They're both such gourmets that I spent the afternoon fussing over hors d'oeuvres and dessert. First, a plate of smoked salmon with purple onions and cucumbers from the garden, arranged in the shape of a flower, as you might have done. An easy dish compared to your recipe for poached pears in cider with whipped cream. Peeling, coring, and quartering the pears turned out to be more of a hassle than I surmised from your playful remark about "preparing the pears (quelle pun)," which made it seem like a breeze. Never having seen that recipe card before, I was also amused by your concluding direction to "serve the pears with hand-whipped cream and auslese or spätlese. Jawohl!" No problem getting the wine, but whipping the cream took much more time and wrist-power than I expected, even using bigger and bigger whisks. Fifteen minutes and five whisks after starting, I was ready for some auslese or spätlese, jawohl, but that was still hours away. Meanwhile, it was a pleasure just to imagine the private bit of pleasure you must have had at that moment, which made me wonder if other such moments might be hidden among your recipe cards. But I didn't have time to look, especially given prep-work for the wild rice and green beans, as well as some research on roasting the leg of lamb. Only then, only then, did I realize that I was preparing almost the same dinner you planned for the day you died. But Ava and Don were so buoyant, the wine he brought so grand, that I kept the secret to myself. Why ruin a perfect meal with a terrible memory?

SUNDAY, OCTOBER 12

Dear Kate,

So much wine last night that I woke with a hangover, and so much rain overnight that I thought — and hoped — the neighborhood picnic would be a washout. But a bright sun and a gentle breeze dried things out, myself included. For the potluck, I put together one of your French potato salads with a tarragon vinaigrette, using the wine vinegar you made last summer. I also contributed some of the bratwurst you bought last fall to share on the charcoal grill. And your festive table cloths as well. So you were there in more ways than one, especially given your founding of the picnic and the park. What I didn't expect is that you'd also turn up in one of the snapshots that Bob took at last fall's picnic and shared with folks today. The last picture that was ever taken of you. And strangely enough, your back was to the camera, as if you were already leaving. I kept that thought to myself, but couldn't help wondering about the coincidence of things, especially after talking with Hannah, who told me that she dreamt of you just a day or two before you died, a dream so premonitory that she regarded it as a farewell. Talk about a destiny that shapes our ends — I can't help thinking of your own remark back in June, just a few months before you died, when Puck tripped you up on the stairs, and the fall momentarily knocked you out — "By all rights," you said, "I should be dead."

SUNDAY, OCTOBER 19

Dear Kate,

The weather today was so mild that I spent the afternoon in your perennial bed. Such a strange combination of things — some aging off like the wild aster, some putting out new growth like the poppies and daylilies, some still in flower like the chrysanthemums — that it's a lovely emblem of past, present, and future, all in the same place at the same time. And a lovely array of fall colors: rusty brown, bright yellow, fading lavender, vivid green, and the sage of Russian sage. But the most striking color was gray — the gray residue of your ashes that I sprinkled around the peony last spring before it started to emerge. How strange to see it there after all these months. And perhaps again next spring. Amy has promised to scatter some of my ashes there when the time comes, so we'll be together again in your perennial bed as well as in Hanalei Bay.

FRIDAY, OCTOBER 24

Dear Kate,

The golden days are ending — snow predicted for Monday night or Tuesday — so I've been putting the yard to bed the past few days. Raking leaves, harvesting vegetables, pulling dead plants, covering marigolds (for one last run of color). Nothing left in the vegetable gardens now but brussels sprouts, swiss chard, radishes, and arugula — the hardy survivors. While digging the last potatoes, I mistakenly thought that today was the eleven-month anniversary of your death, so was more upset than usual, including an outburst of screaming — the first time in several months. But only now that I checked the calendar did I realize it was yesterday. What difference does it make, one day or another? You've been gone for eleven months, give or take a day, and that's what makes all the difference, as I noticed when it came time to do the leaves. Raking them up myself was bad enough — "pale, and hectic red, pestilence-stricken multitudes." But gathering up a tarpful of them and pulling it singlehandedly down to the street — that was worst of all — and not just because of the difficulty, but also because of the memory of us pulling together until they were all spread out along the curb. Back and forth from the terrace to the street — ten times in all I made that trip alone, and by the last time I was talking to myself, muttering in such grief and anger that I went into the house and screamed at your absence, before I remembered your cautionary advice: "Don't go there, don't do that to yourself." And it worked. But then the realization that I hadn't seen anyone the past three days almost started it up again. Talk about self-pity, I'm wallowing in it, but now that the yard work is done, I'll distract myself tomorrow with a day of college football.

MONDAY, OCTOBER 27

Dear Kate,

Going through your papers this morning for the Women's Archives, I came upon a poem about the time you found me in the guest bedroom watching the migratory birds on their way south. A strange coincidence, since they're heading south again right now. The minute I started reading the poem, it took me back to that chilly morning, stunned by the sight of all those birds winging overhead. And by their raucous sound. "Listen," I remember telling you, "listen to them." But I hadn't recalled my tears, until I saw them in your poem. Nor had I realized "some immensity come down between us," until I saw it in your poem. But I do remember how you took my hand in yours and said, "It's early yet, come back to bed awhile."

Now looking back again, I'm torn between your poem and the scene itself, between the moment and what you made of it, between my memory of it and yours. But no matter which I choose, you are its genius, fully in the moment and in possession of it — in your love and in your art. That, I now see, is what I've been seeing ever since you've gone, and for that more than anything else, I'm grateful for your poem. A strange thing, to be so late in seeing what should have been obvious all along. But life, it seems, has a way of obscuring things that only death and art reveal.

FRIDAY, OCTOBER 31

Dear Kate,

Thanks to the cold snap earlier this week, I've spent a few days in-side, answering letters and cards, sending booklets to people who couldn't attend the memorial service, trying to wrap up all that corre-spondence before going to Hawaii. But the past two days, I've been busier than any time since the weekend of your memorial service. All because I let things go too long without doing the storm windows and without getting ready for Halloween. And then, of course, every-thing had to be done at once. Treats for the trickers, pumpkins for the porch, storms for all the windows. No wonder you cursed the window-changing last November, especially the big ones downstairs, too much even for the two of us. Luck was with me, though, when a stranger showed up wanting to see the cold frame–greenhouse you designed in the cellarway — he'd evidently read about it in *Weathering Winter*— so I put him to work helping me with the two biggest win-dows. But Halloween was a job for me alone, and more pleasurable than I imagined, given all the memories of pumpkins past — my scowling faces, your moony smiles. Just to make sure that yours was carved exactly right, I consulted a picture from last year — a picture that I took in late December, thanks to the longevity of your pumpkin, still smiling long after you were gone.

SATURDAY, NOVEMBER 1

Dear Kate,

I was so busy last night with trick-or-treaters that there was hardly time to get maudlin about your absence. Oh yes, I wished you were there, answering the door as always, handing out treats, while I hung back in my owl mask, hooting now and then for the young ones. But my wish was mercifully free of the usual pangs and chills, except for a moment when it was all over, and I wanted to tell you how things had gone. Yet even that was so slight, so swift, that I couldn't help thinking how different it was from my behavior several months ago, when al-most any reminder of you and your cherished holidays could readily unstring me. Now, in fact, I wonder if it was something other than busyness that kept me calm through last night's festivities. Something more profound, like the completion of a cycle — a year of anniversaries without you. Now that Halloween is past, I've gone through every holiday alone, every birthday, every other day of note, except for the day of your death, which I've already relived so many days this year that the memory of it no longer undoes me as it once did. Maybe that's what accounts for everyone's claims about the significance of a year in the passage of grief. So many time bombs exploded that none are left to detonate. Then again, perhaps there's something else going on that I hadn't realized until just now, when it occurred to me that I was doing double duty last night — masked like an owl, hooting at the door, but handing out treats like you. Doing your thing in my own fashion. It probably doesn't sound like a big deal, but the pleasure of last night sure does beat the pain of clinging to things so desperately last December that I tried to keep your last bouquet alive, day after day after day, until three weeks later there was nothing left but a few pale mums in your green glass centerpiece. I didn't say anything about it back then, because I was too embarrassed to mention it. But now I'm happy to report that I've been making my own bouquets and flower arrangements all summer long, and not just with stuff from your perennial bed but also with sunflowers from my vegetable garden. Doing your thing in my fashion. Keeping you alive in ways I never imagined.

TUESDAY, NOVEMBER 4

Dear Kate,

Now I can see why we never traveled in November. So many chores to be done before I go to Hawaii that my knees started acting up again, worse than anytime since I went to the orthopedic surgeon. The past few days, in fact, the left one has gotten so stiff that I can only do the stairs one at a time — little steps for little people. Which makes me wonder how long I can keep living here, though maybe it's just the result of overdoing things and trying to get on without the painkiller, since it evidently counteracts the effect of my daily aspirin. Such, such are the pharmaceutical joys of aging. But maybe I shouldn't complain, given what Trudy's going through. She called this morning with news of an acute stomach or intestinal problem — cancer or a bleeding ulcer — that might keep her from joining me in Hanalei. Yesterday she went to a local emergency room for initial tests, today (when she was supposed to fly here) she'll be seen by her doctor in Manhattan, and

God knows what next. In the middle of that call, I thought of your frustrated prophecy a few years ago when health problems forced her to cancel another trip with us to Hanalei — "I don't think she'll ever join us in Kauai!" And now in a sense your prophecy has come true, now that there's no longer an "us," just a "me." Still, I'm keeping my fingers crossed.

WEDNESDAY, NOVEMBER 5

Dear Kate,

Amy was right about the baggage checkers and your ashes. They went ballistic this morning, the minute they found them in my shoulder bag, especially when I fumbled inside my jacket, looking for the letter of transit from the funeral home. "Step back! Don't move! Put your hands up!" As if they thought I had a gun in my pocket. And then, of course, they all turned sheepish when they realized their mistake, which left me wondering what I would go through in Denver. But Denver had something else in store — a ground fog so dense we were detoured to Grand Junction, along with two dozen other flights. And there we sat on the tarmac for two hours before flying back to Denver, where we sat on the tarmac for another hour before deboarding. So much for my midmorning flight to San Francisco and my afternoon arrival in Lihue. But far from losing my patience, I was fascinated by the cascading complications that produced a virtual gridlock in Denver, airplanes backed up in lines at all the gates. The only thing that troubled me was the prospect of waiting in line to get my flights rebooked. But just then the woman next to me, a bright-eyed, gray-haired math teacher from Bozeman, pulled out her cellphone, called the airline to check on her flight and suggested I do the same to reschedule mine. So before leaving the plane, I had my flights rebooked, to stop over this evening in San Francisco and fly to Hawaii tomorrow morning, then called my brother on the cellphone, arranged to have dinner in the city with him and Phyllis, asked her to book me a room in San Francisco and a few minutes later got a call back on my phone confirming the reservation. How's that for modern life? And then I called Kauai to apprise them of my late arrival. Then Trudy, who told me she'll be arriving early Saturday afternoon. Modern life, indeed!

THURSDAY, NOVEMBER 6

Dear Kate,

Dinner last night in San Francisco was a special treat, and not just because of the succulent roast chicken and the risotto with mushroom-kalamata sauce. Even better was the sight of my brother almost fully recovered, his eyes glittering, his speech almost flawless, giving backseat directions to Phyllis — truly himself again. Before they picked me up, I hardly knew what to expect, given how tenuous he was during the week I visited him after his stroke. Before they picked me up, I also had no idea of how I might feel, for the comparison of his stroke with yours, his outcome with yours, has often been more than I could bear. The feeling sometimes so unpleasant that I couldn't even bring myself to write about it last winter, especially when he was flying here and there as if his life were not at risk. And you, you were gone without a second chance. But last night those feelings were swept away the minute I saw him, his arm outstretched across the years, and his words too — "I still can't believe that she's gone. It's simply unbelievable." Sometimes I think so myself, but the memory of you dying is still so vivid that I understand as never before what it means to say that "seeing is believing."

Seeing the mid-Pacific again and Kauai again and the water offshore, green and blue and purple and turquoise — that too was believing, though it took me back to our first flight in, when the plane banked on its approach and the colors were hard to believe. And so was the land, its strange volcanic upheavals an otherworldly terrain. This time, though, it was suffused with memories all the way north — from the Wailua River and our first night at the Coco Palms to the Hanalei Valley overlook and our first sight of the bay. But I didn't shed a tear, not even at Banana Joe's, where I stocked up on organic vegetables, tropical jam, sea salt, and apple bananas. The only time I almost lost it was driving through the gate of the house itself, and there was Nancy, hose in hand, refreshing the orchids and ti plants. The bear hug she gave me was enough to break the emotional spell, and from then on it was a pleasure to go through all the usual business of putting away the groceries, unpacking my suitcase, and walking the beach at sunset. All I could think of just then was this: "No wonder we came here all those years. No wonder you considered it a spiritual place. No wonder I've come here to scatter your ashes." Back in the house, I unwrapped two framed pictures of you that I brought from Iowa — one in your favorite aloha shirt, the other of you on the Kalalau trail — and put them in the living room. So you're still with me, still with me, in your fashion.

FRIDAY, NOVEMBER 7
Dear Kate,

"How many times can you say goodbye?" That's what Nancy's friend Pam asked last night when she was talking about the last six months of her husband's life. Such a pained expression on her face just then that I finally realized how excruciating it must be when someone's death is a drawn-out affair rather than a swift and sudden end like yours. Saying goodbye again and again and again — it sounds like an incredible torture. But until her outburst, I've often felt bereft not just by your death but by its happening so swiftly we never had a chance to say goodbye. Or so it seemed until I told her your last words to me: "You'll take care of the rice, won't you? And the lamb too?" She smiled and said, "What a lovely parting, and better by far than dying in the middle of an argument." Only then did I realize that you were actually saying goodbye, and so was I in my promise to take care of those things. How strange, that until that realization I took your words at face value, as if you thought there was nothing seriously wrong with you, that the dinner party could go on as planned. Well, who knows what you were thinking, but it now seems that you were leaving things in my hands, expecting me to take care of them in your absence. And so I've tried to do, with the house and the pets and your clothes and your writing and now with your ashes.

I was thinking of your ashes when I stood at the east end of the beach today, looking at the river where we'll board the outrigger next week to scatter them in the bay. Standing there in the spot where you always gathered shells was almost unbearable. But when I turned from the river and looked across the bay, its luminous water, backed by the cloud-topped mountain peaks, sent chills down my arms. A chill of awe rather than anguish, like a recompense for all the others past — just to think of your ashes in that gorgeous place, commingled with the underwater sand. Maybe that's what moved me to write your name in the sand on my way back to the house. I never thought of doing such a thing until I was actually doing it, inscribing the letters with my foot. I got no further than K A before an oncoming wave overtook them, so I moved up the beach a bit and started again, but got no further than K A T E. A few feet further back, and I did your whole name in two-foot-tall letters, K A T E   F R A N K S   K L A U S, just before an even bigger wave rolled in. I wrote your name upon the strand and watched the words dissolve in sand.

Back at the house, Nancy stopped by to visit, and we talked some more — about Pam's grief, your death, the aging coconut palms, your commitment to preserving old trees like those, and the minute I reminded her of your tree projects, she asked, "How would you like to plant a tree here in memory of Kate?" Such a beautiful tribute that I momentarily felt the shivers again. She suggested a papaya. I proposed a mango. So perhaps we'll plant two trees, put some of your ashes under them, and I can check their growth in years to come. Maybe even harvest some fruit if I live long enough.

SATURDAY, NOVEMBER 8
Dear Kate,

On my way to the beach this morning, I saw a rainbow, a rainbow saw I — not a full arc but enough to make me feel the force was definitely with me. It definitely was when I found two pairs of shells completely intact, as well as a few smaller ones, delicately colored — the bounty of high tides. But an hour or so later, back at the house, I got a call from Trudy, still in New Jersey, the pain in her gut so bad that the doctor has scheduled a colonoscopy and endoscopy for Monday and Tuesday, which means she won't be able to get here for more than a few days, if then. She thinks it's ulcers or an inflamed colon from the stress of settling her father's estate. And Amy, whom I called a few minutes later, agrees. Whatever the diagnosis, it's left her feeling guilty at the thought of my being here alone for several more days before everyone arrives. So I did my best to allay her guilt, remembering how you always said, "It's not a useful feeling." And a few words about Nancy being around were enough to do the trick. I also reminded Trudy that she needs to get well in time for her Thanksgiving visit and book-reading at Prairie Lights. When Nancy stopped by this evening and I told her about Trudy not coming, she said, "Don't you think it's probably a good thing you're spending some time here alone before everyone arrives, some time alone in this place where you and Kate used to be together?" And I couldn't disagree, even after being emotionally unstrung this afternoon by a drive out of town when the sun was lighting up the pleated mountain peaks and glowing on the pasture where they hold the farmers' market. I should have known better than to drive there alone after all the times we went there together. But walking into town at lunchtime to do a little shopping and check out the restaurants, I didn't have any problems at all, once I realized that I couldn't possibly dine alone. Best of all, I bought myself a black silk aloha shirt that the young clerk told me I could wear not only to parties but also for dressy occasions at work, and when I told her of my age and retirement, she blurted out, "You seventy-one?! You look like you're in your midfifties!" Now I know what they mean by "island time."

SUNDAY, NOVEMBER 9
Dear Kate,

This morning at low tide, I headed toward the west edge of the bay, and my timing was perfect, for the river crossing was almost completely clear of water. But the waves were still so high at the boulder-edged stretch along the bridge that I couldn't get more than halfway across before turning back for fear of the undertow, especially after I slipped on a rock and heard your cautionary voice — "Get out of there, Klaus, get your head in the game!" How strange, that we used to walk that stretch at low tide without any trouble. And I can still see you gathering shells beyond the bridge, bending over to pick them up where now I can't even keep my footing. The thought of which makes me realize that this apparently stable bay is forever being shaped and reshaped by the tides. You can't step into the same river twice, and you can't step into the same bay twice.

On my way back, I noticed a banquet site being erected under the ironwood grove. Tables and chairs for at least a hundred, a canopy edged with lights, stanchions decorated with ti leaves, torches all around, the head table awash in orchids, the others strewn with dendrobiums. A tropical wedding party extraordinaire! And this evening, I moved a table close to the window to watch the festivities, while savoring a little feast of my own — pan-seared yellow-fin tuna — that I invited Nancy to share with me. Such a glittering scene, torches blazing by the sea, dancing on the beach, that it made a strange backdrop for Nancy's account of her painful childhood. So many woes at the hands of her parents that my orphanhood almost seemed like a piece of good fortune. If only someone could tell a story that might help me become a more grateful widower. But now come to think of it, I've already heard it from Pam.

MONDAY, NOVEMBER 10
Dear Kate,

Do you remember how there were often one or two couples our age, walking the beach when we did, and the mutual recognition of our crossing paths would begin with smiles, move on to hellos, and conclude with us imagining their life stories? Well, it's already happened with a pair who look as if they're the same age as us the last time we were here. He in his late sixties, she in her late fifties. His hair gray, his face tanned like mine, compared to her paler complexion and brown hair like yours. So by degrees I've come to identify with them — have even imagined myself stopping them one morning or afternoon to announce that I too used to walk this beach with my wife, never thinking that our walks would end so soon. But then I wonder what my announcement would lead to — a self-pitying declaration of loneliness, a cautionary bit of advice to seize the day? And the result, of course, is that I keep to myself. This morning, though, was more painful than usual, for even before they approached, I could see them talking in the distance, nodding, gesturing, then suddenly stopping, while he bent over and started drawing something in the sand. Not until I was nearly upon them did I see that he was outlining the façade of a long, one-story house, complete with a front door and windows — a dream place, the vision of a future. Whereas the only thing I could draw in the sand was your name. No future, all past. All I could feel just then was envy, until I noticed a cellphone attached to the side of his swim trunks and wondered what kind of creep would want to be connected on a beach walk? Yes, I too have thought about taking mine along, but I've not yet given in. Nor do I walk bare chested, dangling a t-shirt in my hand. Talk about vanity! Next time we pass, I'll know better.

TUESDAY, NOVEMBER 11

Dear Kate,

Monty and Lizzie arrived this afternoon — she continues to look so much like Monty's side of the family that it's hard to believe she's my granddaughter. Amy and Hannah are due tomorrow, so I stocked up at the farmers' market today. And didn't shed a single tear, thanks to the festive crowd and the tropical crops and a grizzled little fellow selling noni juice, which took me back to the time you peeled a noni and rubbed it on my arm after the poison beetle stung me in Pa'auhau. The sting and the swelling went away so fast that I decided to buy a shot of the stuff today. It's also reputed to be good for arthritis, and who knows what it might do for grief — "It's a panacea," according to Mr. Noni. Such a believer that he's taken its name. Speaking of cure-alls, the thing that's really doing it for me is this place, this perfect half-moon bay — the sway of its palms, the sweep of its tides, the reach of its pleated mountains. Now in their embrace, I walk the beach every morning and afternoon, alone but not without you. Now, in fact, it seems preposterous to have supposed I could ever give up this blessed spot. As if my grief last year were not enough but I needed to compound it by depriving myself of a place where your spirit is with me every step I take. No wonder people talk about grief subverting one's judgment! Now, on the contrary, I'm beginning to think I should come here every year, come at Thanksgiving, as you had proposed, and give thanks for what I find here. This morning, walking in the water by the east edge of the bay, I found a delicately pitted piece of beige coral, shaped like the palm of a hand complete with thumb, as elegant as your diminutive hands. And this afternoon, walking toward the western edge of the bay, I encountered a fisherman, who told me that the boulder-edged stretch of beach where we once gathered shells has been washed out by the surf, "and that's only a hint of what's to come." Though he spoke darkly, he smiled brightly, as double-edged as you.

WEDNESDAY, NOVEMBER 12

Dear Kate,

Amy and I took a beach walk this evening — a sunset stroll when we began, a darkened sky when we returned. Such a stark transition, so disarmingly swift, that I wondered once again about your last afternoon, wondered if you knew you were dying. And who better to ask than Amy, given her nursing experience, her paramedic training, her work with dying patients. An unanswerable question, of course, particularly for someone two thousand miles away from you that afternoon. Yet she put things together in a way that I hadn't thought of before, lighting things up as surely as the glint of the surf. Like a nurse methodically doing a case history, she reminded me of your breast cancer and then the ischemic attack a few years ago — "She got through those things so well, Dad, she probably thought she'd get through this one too. And why not? Just think of all the surgeries she had. She was a survivor, Dad, and survivors don't give up and don't give in to terror, not from what I've seen in the emergency room. Knowing how Kate went at things, I'd bet she was focused completely on getting through — until the hemorrhage overwhelmed her." Just then, I remembered you nodding your head when the doctor asked, "Can you hear me?" And trying without success when he lifted your eyelid and asked, "Can you move your eye over here?" How strange that such a terrible memory should suddenly be so comforting — the image of you so bent upon surviving that you didn't seem to know you were dying. No signs of panic — just the will to survive and then the letting go. The thought of which gives me hope that perhaps I too can let go, if not of the memory, then at least of the anguish that it once aroused. For I've remembered and relived that afternoon so many times since then, pondering every bit of it from start to finish, that I can now think of it without breaking down, especially when I realize that it couldn't have worked out any better than it did. It could easily have worked out much worse. That's what Amy said when we first talked about it last December, and now at last, almost a year later, I see what she meant.

THURSDAY, NOVEMBER 13

Dear Kate,

I've been sleeping the past week on one of the single beds in the back bedroom — a comedown, for sure, from the master bedroom and its big dressing room. But I hardly need all that space compared to Hannah and Monty. So I've put them in the master suite, Amy and Lizzie in the side bedroom. When Martha arrives, I'll offer her the other single bed in the back bedroom with me. That way, Ruth can have the daybed to herself in the living room. In other words, the sleeping arrangements are hunky-dory all around. The only problem is that I haven't been sleeping very well — up and down several times a night, which I first thought was just a matter of jet lag. But now I'm beginning to think it's connected to where I'm sleeping, or perhaps where I'm not sleeping — in the master bedroom with you. A strange turn of events, especially since I don't have any trouble sleeping alone at home. Which makes me think that perhaps it's the single bed that's giving me trouble, and not just because I don't have enough room to twist and turn in my sleep. Even awake, I don't feel comfortable about the idea of sleeping in a single bed. Ain't it funny, that a little thing like that could make such a big difference. But it's also the case that I haven't slept in a single bed since I was in my bachelor apartment, some forty years ago. The memory of which made me realize something today that I hadn't quite realized before — namely, that I'm now a single man once again. "So what else is new?" you might ask — I've been single, in fact, since the day you died. Yet until quite recently, I've often been so beset by grief that I've been inclined to think of myself and talk of myself as if my fate were still bound up with yours, as if it were still "Kate and I," when in truth it's I alone. Oh yes, you're still there inside me and always will be until I shuffle off this mortal coil. But the harsh truth — so harsh that I've evidently been reluctant to see it or say it as plainly as this — is that I'm on my own. It's a bracing truth as well, a challenge of sorts, to be on my own and make something of it, as you would have. So, after all, I'm grateful to have been here alone the past week, alone on this remote speck of land, walking the beach by myself while some walk hand in hand.

FRIDAY, NOVEMBER 14

Dear Kate,

If I could spirit you back for a day, it would have been today, so you could hear Martha ooh-ing and aah-ing all the way north from the airport to the house. And the minute she saw the bay, exclaiming like it was the climax of a sacred pilgrimage. Just as you always predicted, she fell in love with the place at first sight, so much so that by bedtime she was already imagining a new life on Kauai for Lynn and herself, complete with jobs and a house and God knows what else. "A friend of mine told me," she said, "that once I see Hanalei Bay, I'll never want to leave, and he was right." Actually, it was touching to see how deeply moved she was by the natural beauty of the place, as if she finally understood why we'd been coming here the past twenty years. Now my only fear is that she and Lynn might not be able to find jobs like those they have in Florida. But who am I to throw water on her dreams, having come here myself more often than I could ever have imagined.

And she's not the only one who's been swept away. Hannah and Monty, too, even though they honeymooned here some twenty years ago, but were evidently so cocooned by the resort that they never really savored the place as they're doing now. Now, everyone's walking the bay, morning and afternoon, just as you did. And relishing my home-cooked dinners, just as you did, especially the pan-seared ahi. And Monty's found such beautiful shells that each day he's been leaving a few of special choice by your picture in the living room, so he's turned it into a shrine in honor of the presiding spirit. By a happy coincidence, your eyes are cast slightly downward, and you've got a sly smile on your face, as if you were looking at the shells with an air of approval. So I've added a few of my own for good measure.

FRIDAY, NOVEMBER 15

Dear Kate,

Talk about sacred offerings — Ruth arrived this morning, and no sooner did I pick her up at the airport and welcome her with a Micronesian-ginger lei than she directed me to a local woman who had made six puakinikini leis on special order. One for each of us to wear today and then fling into the sea tomorrow morning when we scatter your ashes. How's that for island extravagance? According to Ruth, puakinikini are a traditional offering, and I can see why, given their elegant tubelike flowers and pungent aroma. Those six plus the leis that Monty and Lizzie brought and the ones I gave to Martha and Ruth will all be flung in the bay tomorrow. And you thought that no one would care? But the leis and even the special prayer she'll read, written for the occasion by Pua, are nothing compared to the presence of Ruth herself, come from Oahu just to honor you. She's now eighty, believe it or not, and still as laid back as when we first met her more than twenty years ago. Now, if only I can learn to bear up as she has in the wake of

George's death, sauntering around in that inimitable way of hers, got up today in a Greek fisherman's cap, a jaunty sweatshirt, and nothing for luggage but a little black shoulder bag and a folder containing her prayer.

She showed me the prayer, as if she wanted to be sure that I approved, and I was touched to see that it's based on your Thanksgiving prayer, which I sent her last year, but never imagined that she and Pua would turn it into something like this:

> Lord, we thank you
> For the precious gift you spread before us
> For Kate's life
> And for her stay within the company of loved ones
> All around her.

Such an evocative reworking of yours, especially together with Pua's Hawaiian version of it, that I felt a bit timid about showing her my prayer, which is also based on one from your past (and mine):

> Now we've laid you down to sleep,
> I pray the Lord your soul to keep,
> Until my own comes here to sleep,
> I pray the Lord your soul to keep.
> And when we're here amid the deep,
> I pray the Lord our souls to keep.
> And when we're here amid the deep,
> I pray the Lord our souls to keep.

I figured you wouldn't want anything lavish, so I tried to keep it as short and simple as possible. Theologians, of course, would probably be outraged by my tacit confusion of one's ashes with one's soul. But it says what I feel most moved to pray for. And as you can see, it's based on the assumption that my ashes will also be scattered in the bay. Amy has promised to mix them with a handful of yours that she's saved. So, after all, we'll be together in the sweet bye-and-bye. Meanwhile, with Amy's help, I just finished dividing your ashes into two Ziploc bags (one for each outrigger), with a handful left over for the tree planting on Monday. How strange to be divvying you up like that, but then again how delightful to think of you in all your favorite places — here in Hawaii and back in Iowa too.

SUNDAY, NOVEMBER 16

Dear Kate,

We gathered at sunrise, the first time since I arrived without the early morning showers. A good omen, but all of us were a bit on edge about the outriggers, and more than a bit uncertain about the ceremony itself. You, of course, would have been herding us along, forever the camp counselor, always certain of how things should be done and how they'd work out. But all I could think of as we stood around in the kitchen, sipping our juice, was the urgency of doing it right, whatever that might mean, especially since I'd been waiting almost a year to do it, and no second chances to get it right. Then, for the first time in my life, I understood the value of ritual and formalized ceremony, for here we were about to perform your last rites without any script to guide us, except for the prayers that Ruth and I had written. Oh yes, we were all got up in our best canoeing gear. "She would have expected nothing less," is the way that Martha put it. But the beautiful rockfish t-shirt that Hannah and Monty had given me some ten years ago, that I was wearing for the first time as if I'd been saving it all those years just for this morning — it was hardly enough to keep me from feeling that we were all on a high lonesome, about to embark on a venture that could well end up leaving us all very deeply depressed.

The minute we got to the river's edge and met Barbara and Richard, our hosts from the Hanalei Canoe Club, I could see that at least we were in very good hands, especially after they gave us a lesson in paddling and in sitting correctly so as not capsize the boat ("Pull the paddle straight down and back, straight down and back. Lean toward the outrigger, don't lean away! Lean toward the outrigger, not toward the canoe!"). The mere thought of rolling over, otherwise known as a "huli" (not to be confused with the hula), was enough to keep those rules in mind from start to finish. Then after meeting the other crew members and watching them launch the canoes, we boarded the narrow boats — Hannah, Martha, and I in one, Amy, Ruth, Monty, and Lizzie in the other — and began to row downriver into the bay, guided by the masterly directions and rowing of the crew. Given your days of canoeing on the Wapsipinicon, you'd have loved the discipline, especially the methodical switching of paddles from one side to the other every twelve strokes. Just your sort of rigorous thing, a cadence to keep us in balance. So sleek and smooth at first, thanks to being in the channel, that it felt as if we were gliding on silk, transported not by our own efforts but by a spirit within the river. Or so it seemed, until we met the crosscurrent and swell of the ocean, buoying us up so fast I shuddered to think how quickly we could be buoyed into a huli. Wouldn't it be ironic, I thought just then, if I wound up in the water, dogpaddling for dear life, your ashes still in hand? But just as quickly we moved beyond the swell into calmer waters, circling in a wide arc to arrive at the pier for some snapshots by Nancy, before heading out to the center of the bay, where I was momentarily transfixed by the spread of the mountain range, never having seen it from that angle. Like an echo of the bay and a dramatic backdrop for our ceremony.

Then with a brief signal from Richard, we began. I put my hand in the Ziploc bag, pulled out a fistful of your ashes and gradually released them with a backward swoop of my arm across the water — a brief gray streak, widening before they started to sink — and passed the bag to Martha, who cast a handful upon the water and passed the bag to Hannah, who passed it back to Martha, who passed it back to me. Back and forth another time before our bag was done. Streak after streak after streak. And the same in the other boat, just a few yards away. But the streaks were nothing compared to the ghostly clouds that we suddenly noticed descending through the pellucid water, as if your ashes were coming to life, expanding and taking form, one cloud after the other energized by the sea, as if they, as if you, were swimming to the depths, to your final resting place. Until suddenly they were so deep we could hardly see them at all. And then, as if I'd known all along what to do, I took off my lei and cast it upon the water, then Martha flung hers, and Hannah hers, and the others theirs. Lei upon lei upon lei upon the waters. Such a casting of beauteous things, you'd probably have considered it a wretched (and splendid) excess. And then as the leis were floating upon the water, Ruth offered her prayer, and she delivered it not only in English but also in Hawaiian — such a haunting sound that I'll never forget it. For a moment, I was so moved by the resonance of the Hawaiian words that I didn't want to read my English prayer, but something within me, the likes of which I've never felt before, suddenly started uttering the words, and soon enough I was done. And so too I thought the ceremony was done, until Richard invited us to spend a few moments of silence reflecting on the service and our memories of you. How strange that all I could think of just then was how furious you'd be if you knew that such a thing were being done without your having a hand in the planning, performance, and ultimate direction of it. The dramatist's last production. The only other thing I felt was a great sense of relief, greater than at any other time this year, as if a huge burden had fallen away from me. Your ashes finally laid to rest in a service so beautiful that it perfectly befit you, in a spot so dazzling it's no wonder that Richard said, "There's no better place to spend eternity." And then, as if on command from somewhere on high, there appeared in that cloudless blue sky, directly over the mountains, stage center, a full rainbow arcing down into the water beyond us, as if you were suddenly with us, having the last word. A rainbow without rain. Such a miraculous thing that I'm shivering again just thinking of it.

In the wake of that apparition, of course, everything else was anticlimactic. So I won't bother you with the details except to report that I did exactly what you would have expected and took everyone to a celebratory champagne brunch at the Hanalei Café, where we feasted on another view of the bay, looking down from above at where we'd been just a few hours before, the waves glistening, the doves fluttering on our table, the palms swaying in the distance, and Bali Ha'i beyond. And then spent the rest of the day recovering from the feast.

MONDAY, NOVEMBER 17

Aloha, Kate,

First thing this morning, we planted a tree in memory of you. Actually, we didn't do the planting. Scott did it. Scott, landscaper and tree man extraordinaire. And we, we were not as many as yesterday. Amy and Martha had taken Ruth to the airport. Hannah, Monty, and Lizzie were out walking the beach. So it was just Nancy and I — she there to show him the exact site for the tree, in the front corner right between the two lemon trees. I standing by with a handful of your ashes to put in the bottom of the tree hole. Not that the others didn't care. It's just that we didn't know exactly when he'd show up, and it didn't seem as if there'd be anything special to see. But no sooner did he arrive than the fireworks began, for Scott is a high-energy sort of guy — so driven in his work and so passionately committed to his trees that he seems out of place in this laid-back world of orchids and surfers. The sort of person you'd have craved as a cohort when you were planning and planting the heritage grove. So knowledgeable and no-nonsense that the first thing he announced was "No papaya. And no mango either. They don't do well in the salt air. Too close to the water. Probably would live only a few years in this spot, which certainly wouldn't be a good memorial for your wife." So much for my fanciful vision of plucking memorial fruit in years to come. But Scott had something better in the back of his truck — a magnificent red heliconia, its flower stalk so striking and erotic I could hardly believe it. Better still, it'll keep flowering and renewing itself for years on end, like other members of the banana tree family to which it belongs.

He dug a goodly hole, as you always did, spading it out nonstop, nonstop, then worked in some slow-release fertilizer, quickly, quickly, then suddenly stepped back and away, silently waiting for me to scatter your ashes in the bottom of the hole, before he moved back in and set the tree right on top of them. Your ashes, the tree. A marriage below ground. Then the backfilling, the tamping, and finally a mulch of koa wood chips. "Those are koa wood chips," he said, three or four times over, as proud of his chips as you of your koa wood bracelets and bowls. But the tree itself is what really got me and everyone else — its pale green leaves, its tall and slender shape, like a tropical tree-form version of you. Monty took pictures of it. Martha plans to do a painting of it.

It's now only six feet tall, but according to Scott will soon reach fifteen or twenty feet. So I've given Nancy a disposable camera and asked her to take a monthly snapshot. Meanwhile, I couldn't stop visiting it today, just to see its pale green leaves, luminous in the sun. There you are, Kate. There you are. And there in the bay as well. So I know where to find you on land or sea whenever I return. And return I will — next Thanksgiving and every Thanksgiving until I'm with you in the sweet bye-and-bye.

Aloha, Kate. Aloha nui loa.

Afterword

The first year, so they say, is the hardest. Survive it, and the pain is not so intense or frequent as before — a truth I can certainly vouch for, now that two years have passed since Kate was swept away. Here I am in Hanalei again, here with everyone who came last year to scatter her ashes, and though the sadness persists, I've hardly shed a tear or felt a shiver, except at the first sight of the heliconia, twice as big as when we planted it last year, and then at the first sight of the bay, her restless resting place. Even today, the two-year anniversary of her death, I walked the bay and walked the bay again, overcome by nothing so much as the dazzle of its surf, a sudden downpour, and a double rainbow — as if in memory of her passing and of the rainbow that graced our ceremonies last year. Time and tide do, after all, have a way of healing, though the healing itself is troubling. Not a day goes by that I don't think of Kate or invoke one of her sayings or mention her to someone or do something inspired by her example, and not a day goes by that I don't feel troubled by my less-troubled state of mind. How can it be that she gave me thirty-seven years of her love, and I only a single year of intense mourning? Sometimes, I think it was the letters — a year of writing them and another year of putting them in book form. Daily therapy that no therapist could match. So, when people ask how I survived the shock, I often talk of the letters as having kept me sane, as if I avoided madness by writing my way out of grief, even as I relived the grief of that year in the process of condensing it for this book. But I also have to acknowledge that my anguish was lessened by the companionship of a person who entered my life this year — a woman I'd known and admired from afar who left a message on my answering machine, inviting me to see *Calendar Girls*, a bosomy bit of wisdom about seizing the day that surely would have captivated Kate. And so I seized it. How strange, though, to be on the receiving end of something I never sought, especially after telling Bob and Carol and Hannah and Trudy and myself that I'd never get involved again. Everyone here tells me to embrace my good fortune. But I can't help wondering what Kate would have thought and said. "So much for your undying love"? Or, "This is the flower that you have, you don't have the other"? Talk about confusion! And even without knowing what Kate might think, I know how puzzled I often feel, loving her as I continue to do, even as I now love someone who loves me in part for my devotion to Kate. Nothing, after all, is clear-cut and definite, except for the truth of her poignant refrain — "Don't you realize how little time we have?" So, in this season of thanksgiving, I consider myself doubly blessed (and bemused) by the memory of her love and by the love that now engulfs me.

Life after death, as Kate might have said, is here and here alone.

C. H. K.
Hanalei, Hawaii
NOVEMBER 23, 2004

Sightline Books
The Iowa Series in Literary Nonfiction

The Men in My Country
MARILYN ABILDSKOV

Shadow Girl: A Memoir of Attachment
DEB ABRAMSON

Embalming Mom: Essays in Life
JANET BURROWAY

Fauna and Flora, Earth and Sky: Brushes with Nature's Wisdom
TRUDY DITTMAR

Letters to Kate: Life after Life
CARL H. KLAUS

Essays of Elia
CHARLES LAMB

The Body of Brooklyn
DAVID LAZAR

No Such Country: Essays toward Home
ELMAR LUETH

Currency of the Heart: A Year of Investing, Death, Work, and Coins
DONALD R. NICHOLS

Memoirs of a Revolutionary
VICTOR SERGE

The Harvard Black Rock Forest
GEORGE W. S. TROW